ADVANCE PRAISE

"The EQ Deficiency is unlike any emotional intelligence book I have read. It approaches EQ from a different angle and, it's given me a new perspective on communication, my perception of others, and the power of awareness."

— ANDREW ROBERTS, DIRECTOR, WELLS FARGO

"Really great! I was able to apply much of what I learned immediately and found myself thinking about how I can be agile for future interactions and meetings to drive the idea of what is possible for my teams. I found myself both motivated and hopeful."

— BLAIR PRIMIS, SENIOR VP, MARKETING & TALENT MANAGEMENT, ORTHOCAROLINA

"...Upon graduation, we find out, life is not a high school or college textbook and something was missing from our toolbox. Brittney-Nicole Connor-Savarda provides that missing blueprint for us to tap into our emotional intelligence to guide us through the twists and turns life throws at us. The EQ Deficiency is a must read in order to live life to its fullest."

— DARYL DAVIS, INTERNATIONAL BLUES MUSICIAN, ACTIVIST

"At the root of all communication challenges lives the EQ factor. This book dives into those challenge and forces us to take a closer look at how we lead, parent, & partner. Those who are struggling to build stronger, more meaningful connections should pick up this book and get to work."

— STACY CASSIO, FOUNDER & CEO, PINK MENTOR NETWORK

"Our society has become self-centered and, quite frankly, immature. In this book, Brittney-Nichole shares her skills, knowledge and experience to allow us to understand how we got here, and more importantly, how we can get to a better place. The EQ Deficiency is a must read for anyone who cares."

— DR. HENRY DEPHILLIPS, PHYSICIAN EXECUTIVE

"Anyone on the pathway to self-awareness and whose importance is being effective with people and situations should definitely read The EQ Deficiency. This booked has not only opened my eyes but has also validated so many areas of life to me. It's an easy read and important in the journey of self-enlightenment."

— CHERISE WALKER, VP, TALENT PARTNERSHIPS & TALENT INSIGHTS, OPERATIONS DIRECTOR, CHARLOTTE ALLIANCE FOUNDATION

The EQ Deficiency

How Emotional Intelligence and Compassion Can Cure an Emotional Pandemic, Solve Our "People Problems" and Be a Catalyst for Positive Change

Brittney-Nichole Connor-Savarda
Founder of Catalyst 4 Change LLC; Generation EQ

23rd Realm Publishing

To Request permission, contact the publisher at 23rdrealmpublishing@gmail.com

LIBRARY OF CONGRESS-IN-PUBLICATION DATA
Connor-Savarda, Brittney-Nichole
The EQ deficiency: how emotional intelligence and compassion can cure an emotional pandemic, solve our "people problems "and be a catalyst for positive change /
LCCN: 202914706

Brittney-Nichole Connor-Savarda
Hardback: 9781734732825
Paperback: 9781734732801
Ebook: 9781734732818

First paperback edition September 2020

Edited by Steven Rigolosi and Sarah Busby
Cover art and illustrations by Brittney-Nichole Connor-Savarda
Layout by Brittney-Nichole Connor-Savarda

Printed in the USA.

23rd Realm Publishing
a division of Catalyst 4 Change LLC
Charlotte, NC

DEDICATION:

In loving memory of my grandfather and friend:

Charles (Pete) Franklin Connor
(1927-2017)

"We cannot tell what may happen to us in the strange medley of life. But we can decide what happens in us—how we can take it, what we do with it—and that is what really counts in the end."

—Joseph Fort Newton

CONTENTS

Acknowledging the Situation

Ten years ago, I was in pain. Emotional pain. I had been suffering from anxiety for years, but it wasn't until I was in a new relationship, in a new city, and around new people, that I came to realize I was the common problem.

Once I recognized my unhappiness and discomfort was far greater than any pain I would feel from facing my demons, I was on a mission to be a happier and emotionally healthier person, no matter how long it took—and it took some time. In fact, I am still growing and developing. And it has been worth every unpleasant self-discovery, confession (not in a religious sense), and all the (hard to swallow) feedback from others.

When I think back to the person I was ten years ago, compared to the person I am today, writing this book, they are so vastly different that it's hard to identify with the "old Brittney." Although I don't identify with who I used to be and how I used to act, I am not ashamed of that younger, lost, and angry version of myself. I feel for her and I thank her. Because of her struggles, life experiences, and emotional suffering, I am able to appreciate the little things, take responsibility for the things I felt I had no control over, and develop the knowledge and understanding of the human psyche and emotions that I can now share with the world.

I often reflect on that time in my life and wonder, "How did I manage to live that way for so long?" I spent 23-years trapped and controlled by my emotions. In those moments, I felt the most miserable feelings I have felt in my life so far. It was a feeling of utter despair. The most blood-curdling scream you can imagine, could never do justice to the noise and turbulence I felt on the inside. A feeling of control, choice, and pleasure could disappear in an instant.

When despair turned to panic, it was as if the oxygen was drained from the room, as I struggled to catch my breath. My body started to have withdrawals from reality. I imagined that, if there was a hell, it couldn't possibly be worse than the way I felt in those moments.

I felt like a teacup that had been broken several times and badly glued back together—the glue being my ego which forced me to hide my imperfections out of shame.

But, for us to grow and develop, we must break away from old habits and ways of thinking. We must put our egos on the shelf—no easy task. Without it, we crumble and feel broken. The key is to cherish our broken pieces, not to try to "fix" what is broken and make it appear perfect. By accepting and repurposing those pieces, we can transform them into a new and beautiful mosaic of our lives. This is one of many things developing my emotional intelligence has taught me.

I wear these scars with pride because I know all my hardships made me who I am today. When we overcome difficulties in our life and look back, there is so much we can learn from our experiences.

I now have the privilege to help others. Not simply because I have a degree in psychology, but because I have lived it. My degree only helps me to reinforce this insight with an understanding of the science and complexity of the human mind.

I have been eager to write a book for a couple of years now. I put it off because the thought of 200 plus pages seemed daunting. The first strong urge occurred while I was still working a full-time job, in two leadership positions in outside nonprofits, and in the infancy of launching my business, Catalyst 4 Change LLC. I had all burners lit with no room to add yet another time-consuming task. Looking back, it wouldn't have been the best time, regardless of how full my plate was. I wasn't ready. I have learned and changed so much in those few years.

I told myself that, once I left my full-time job, I would have more time to focus on my book. But other things seemed to fill the gaps and it was put on the shelf yet again. It was only after returning from my honeymoon, and having two weeks of no meetings or engagements, that the thought of writing the book resurfaced. There was a sea of emotions regarding recent events, politics, and rants on social media that pushed me to get started.

My hope is that this book brings you clarity as to why we behave and think the way we do, and how to overcome the unpleasant emotions and situations that many of us face every day. More importantly, it will give you a better understanding of emotional intelligence as the key to unlock growth and self-development.

First, however, we must understand the concept itself: What is emotional intelligence?

What is EQ and Why Does It Matter?

In a world riddled with egocentrism, hair-trigger impulse, Twitter wars, social media rants, cultural and political polarization, and chronic anxiety and depression, humanity desperately needs a solution to our "people problems".

While writing this book, the world is experiencing a pandemic (COVID-19), which has overwhelmed the global economy, and drastically altered how we interact and operate in our personal and professional lives. Millions have lost their jobs or become ill; loneliness and social isolation—already an epidemic in our society—are worsened by the need to socially distance; and all of us are dealing with unprecedented stress and anxiety in these uncertain times.

While we may not have control over how our government and leaders handle the situation, or how it affects our jobs and the economy, we do have the ability to control how we choose to react and cope. Unfortunately, as a collective society, we lack the skills and understanding to effectively manage these emotions. And, in times of crisis, this deficit in EQ stands out more than ever before.

Our lack of emotional intelligence is a pandemic in itself. Day in and day out, we mimic the social scripts that tell us how we should think, act, and what we should believe, with little regard as to why. Our interactions with others are often set to autopilot, with everyday exchanges like "how are you?" and "I'm fine" that carry little to no genuine interest. And our impulsive and hateful outbursts and lack of respect and tolerance for the alternative perspectives of other cultures and beliefs are justified through our narrow perspective of reality. We are suffering both individually and as a collective society.

The cure to all these issues can be found in developing our emotional intelligence and compassion.

In this book we will first look at the symptoms of this EQ deficiency, why we think and behave in the ways that we do, and learn the strategies and mindset shifts needed to catalyze positive change in the world. Let's first look at the evolution of emotional intelligence as a psychological theory.

UNDERSTANDING EMOTIONAL INTELLIGENCE

The term emotional intelligence was coined by psychologist Peter Salovey and John Mayer (not the musician) back in 1990. They describe emotional intelligence as a "Form of social intelligence that involves the ability to monitor one's own and others' feelings and emotions, to discriminate among them, and to use this information to guide one's thinking and action."[1]

Depending on the institution, psychologist, or philosopher, the structure or components of emotional intelligence and the terms used may vary ever so slightly. This book uses five components that are in alignment with Daniel Goleman's definition of emotional intelligence:

Self-awareness: accurately defining your emotions, the origins of those emotions, and the effects those emotions have on yourself and the people around you; the ability to know your personal strengths and limits; the ability to accurately assess how others perceive your behavior.

Self-regulation: managing your emotions and behavioral state; taking responsibility for your actions; being open to change and innovation.

Motivation: directing emotions that guide you to reach your goals; dedication in achieving your goals despite obstacles or setbacks.

Social Skills: the ability to lead, change, build trust, communicate effectively, collaborate, and cooperate with others; ability to sense the synergy of a group and adapt accordingly.

Empathy: understanding and sharing the emotions of others; ability to assess other people's needs.[2]

Emotional intelligence does not discriminate amongst demographics. Someone can be poor and have a high EQ, while the CEO of a Fortune 100 company, making millions of dollars, may have a very low EQ. Being "successful," in the sense of being rich or in a high position of authority, does not mean you are emotionally intelligent. In addition, emotional intelligence—also known as EQ (emotional quotient) or EI for short—is a skill that can be developed and does not correlate to IQ (intelligence quotient) which tends to "max out" around our early twenties. Studies show that the most respected leaders, along with 90% of top performers, have high EQs.[3]

Developing our social-emotional literacy (SEL)—the knowledge and use of emotional intelligence—does not mean that our core beliefs will necessarily change (although they could if you choose to change them). It does mean, however, that we will not allow our emotions and strongly held beliefs to be used against us or allow our ego to present our opinion as fact. Developing our SEL allows us to have more productive conversations and see other points of view more clearly. Without EQ it becomes difficult—if not impossible—to connect and empathize with individuals who hold different beliefs than our own. Being emotionally intelligent does not mean that we will avoid unpleasant emotions such as anger, frustration, or sadness. Emotions, pleasant and unpleasant, are here to stay. However, as you develop your EQ, you should notice a significant decrease in unpleasant emotions as well as their level of intensity.

Like any skill, emotional intelligence is developed through practice. We wouldn't hire or trust a surgeon who only read about human anatomy in textbooks and watched videos of surgeries being performed. Successfully building and acting on emotional intelligence requires a combination of developing a solid foundation of knowledge about the subject, consistently applying it in our lives, and constantly tweaking and fine-tuning it.

I have structured this book very differently than most books around emotional intelligence. Instead of simply defining what emotional intelligence is and how to develop it, (through qualitative analysis) I have provided a broader perspective on how the human mind behaves, why we have shortcomings and, in addition, how to identify with others based on how they are communicating and reacting to us.

By the end of this book you should be able to better understand why we have human discord; develop a high level understanding of how the human mind operates—which helps us to be more empathetic to our own shortfalls— and how to develop your own emotional intelligence—relieving stress, anxiety, depression and many other symptoms of low EQ. Finally, you should be able to see a clear path toward becoming a catalyst for positive change.

The EQ Deficiency

PART 1

HOW DID WE GET HERE?

1

Introducing
the EQ Deficiency

"We are dangerous when we are not conscious of our responsibility for how we behave, think, and feel."

— Marshall B. Rosenberg

Humanity is facing an emotional crisis, which I call the *EQ Deficiency* — a lack in emotional awareness and understanding of how our thoughts and behaviors correlate with overall well-being, connection, performance, and understanding of the world beyond our perceived reality. Symptoms may include, but are not limited to:

- Emotional outburst
- Low self-esteem
- Poor performance
- Lack of empathy
- Micromanagement
- Poor listening skills
- Unproductive conflict
- Leadership by fear
- Intimidation
- Scapegoating
- Social polarization
- Miscommunication
- Belittling others

- Depression
- Anxiety
- Violence
- Loneliness
- Defensiveness
- Contempt
- Self-loathing
- Egocentrism
- Projection
- Denial
- Abuse
- Intolerance
- Isolation

Some may argue the internet, social media, and an increasingly demanding lifestyle are the causes of this unprecedented outbreak of emotional instability. I disagree. I believe our society lacks a strong and supportive social-emotional infrastructure, resulting from a lack of understanding and awareness of the human psyche and the powerful role our mind-set and emotions play in our daily lives.

Breakneck advancements in technology have allowed for swift globalization, previously unthinkable innovations, and easy access to multicultural connections. The evolution of human thought and behavior is struggling to catch up.

For generations, and presumably since the dawn of humanity, dominance, human intellect (IQ), and conforming to social norms have been seen as the foundation for our survival and successes. As such, these characteristics have been baked into the structure of society. However, a revolution has begun, as humanity is awakening to the capabilities of the human mind and, in particular, emotional intelligence and raised consciousness. We now realize our emotions are at the heart of every thought and decision, and are a driving force in business, relationships, commerce, law, religion, and economics.

Given that emotions play a major role in our day-to-day life, isn't it ironic that they are absent in the curriculums of our educational systems and in the structure of most societies? And yet, "soft skills" such as adaptability, empathy, communication, collaboration, authenticity, and self-management are highly coveted in organizations and desperately needed in leadership (organizational and diplomatic).

Consumed by our fast-paced lives, we don't take the time to check in with our and others' emotions. We are on autopilot, governed by egocentric social norms and centuries of behavioral conditioning. When the stakes are high and we feel threatened, rules and values are easily hijacked by primitive emotional impulses, which override rational processing. Logic and intellect are not enough. We must develop deeper emotional ties to the people and environment around us—compassion, empathy, and understanding—if we are to overcome the social and contextual challenges we face today.

This book aims to break down *why* we do, say, act, and react in the ways we do. It explores the current emotional state of humanity, and how we can evolve into more productive, cooperative, and emotionally intelligent beings. Without being fully aware of our behaviors and feelings, and without the ability to regulate them, we are mere puppets, unaware of the manipulative influence of modern society, and prisoners of our own emotions.

Increasing our EQ generates immense benefits. Individuals with high EQ make up 90% of top performers, have a greater sense of well-being and mental clarity, are more likely to be financially stable and physically healthier, are more effective at managing tasks and their time, and more emotionally resilient during uncertain and difficult circumstances.

Intangible skills like self-awareness and regulation can generate significant tangible value. In 2009, TalentSmart examined the emotional intelligence of 42,000 workers across various industries and found individuals with high emotional intelligence averaged $29,000 more a year in salary.[4]

While an individual's IQ may increase just a few points over extended periods of time, their EQ proficiency has the potential to increase dramatically. Although there is not yet a standardized test for scoring EQ, if an individual (hypothetically speaking) scores 27 points out of a possible 100, it is not unrealistic to assume they could increase their score to the maximum of 100 points.

The importance of intellect should not be dismissed; however, EQ can be thought of as a turbocharger, accelerating and maximizing our full potential, fostering a more fulfilling life for ourselves and enriching the lives of others around us. With enough of us practicing and embracing emotional intelligence, we can alter the emotionally turbulent climate we are living in today.

2

Emotional Turbulence in an Era of Innovation

"We are a society of notoriously unhappy people: lonely, anxious, depressed, destructive, dependent—people who are glad when we have killed the time, we are trying so hard to save."

— Erich Fromm, *To Have or to Be? The Nature of the Psyche*

While sitting in a local Italian bistro, nestled in the heart of Tuscany, sipping her latte, sociologist, Dr. Melanie Baugh, couldn't help but notice the family of five sitting just a few tables away. A mother, father, and their three children—all with their heads bowed down, peering into the screens of their devices, as if entranced. While trying not to stare, Baugh couldn't help but wonder, "How long will it take before someone looks up and makes eye contact or sparks a conversation?"

Roughly ten minutes into her observation, the youngest child taps the ceramic vessel of cream with the edge of her tablet, causing the container to tip ever so slightly, and creating a clinking sound alerting the mother. The mother lifts her eyes only long enough to slide the cream out of reach from the child and continues to engage with her phone. No eye contact or verbal communication occurs between mother and daughter.

Only minutes prior to leaving did the adults lower their devices to scan the table, collect their things, and leave. All three children walked out the door of the cafe with devices still in hand and eyes fixated on the screens.

To Baugh's right, sat a couple who (like her) appeared to be vacationing. They laughed and smiled, took a few selfies together, and then proceeded to take picture after picture after picture, as if to get the perfect angle of their Caffè correttos and biscotti. The man, by suggestion of the young woman, began taking—not so candid— "candids" of her as she gazed blissfully into nothingness, as if to ponder the unknown wonders of the universe. Baugh watched as the young woman fluffed her hair, pouted her lips, tilted her head from side to side, and darted her eyes in various directions. As the man passed the phone back to her, she carefully reviewed the "photo shoot." Evidently unsatisfied, she passed the phone back for several more rounds of poses and reviews. After several bouts of this back and forth, she retrieved her phone and began to tap away at her screen. This, Baugh imagined, was the young women promoting her "experience" on social media for the world to see.

What Baugh witnessed in this quaint Tuscan bistro is a common global phenomenon. We are a society who yearns for connection and fulfillment in life, but we lack an understanding of how to achieve such contentment in order to experience the richness that life has to offer.

Throughout the centuries, our primary focus has been in high IQ fields of study such as STEM (science, technology, engineering, and mathematics), while little attention has been given to the value of psychological health and the power of emotional control.

As a result, we have a society filled with new technologies and innovations and yet we lack the fundamental skills to understand and control our emotions, cooperate with one another, and harness the power of combining both IQ and EQ to optimize our full potential. Without control and understanding of the mind—the mind that has enabled this human innovation—the ways in which we use these innovations can be harmful to ourselves and others.

EQ DEFICIENCY MEETS THE 21ST CENTURY

If we were to observe a graph depicting the history of human technology, we would see a long and subtle (almost nonexistent) rise that spans thousands of years, followed by a very sharp and fast ascent to the technological advancements of today. Never before has one generation lived to witness and experience so many innovations. It took 97 years to go from a landline telephone to the first cellular telephone. Only ten years later, the Internet was born. Since the birth of the Internet, technology has accelerated ever more rapidly.

The Greatest Generation (born in the 1920s-1930s) saw some of the most substantial change in technological advancement than any other generation in current history. Many were born to households without indoor plumbing and some without electricity. Yet, this same generation witnessed the first moon landing, the internet, smartphone technology, virtual reality and the onset of artificial intelligence.

Since the turn of the 21st century, new technologies have altered the ways and the rate at which we digest and produce information, conduct business, assess and debate politics, entertain ourselves and others, find service providers (and become service providers for others), make purchases, and communicate with family, friends, and foes.

While these technologies were created to assist, connect, and advance humanity; psychologically, we were not prepared. This rapid succession in innovation has not been met with the same progress in human behavior and evolution. As a society, we still face the same personal and diplomatic challenges we faced centuries ago. While we have made some progress in human rights, diversity and inclusion, it is still a constant battle, with the scale shifting slowly and only ever so slightly toward progress.

Without an increase in emotional intelligence, technology's potential for good can instead become an outlet for toxic expression, a distraction from and exaggeration of reality, directing our attention away from introspection and living in the moment. This deficit in EQ sets us on a path to self-destruction if we do not change our ways. Humanity is in the midst of a serious social-emotional crisis. The symptoms of our EQ deficiency could fill several books by themselves.

Before we dive in to how to overcome our conundrum, let's look at a few examples of how a deficit of EQ shows up in our daily lives, ranging from minor distraction and unease, to fatal consequences. I have narrowed it down to a few situations we often face in today's world.

CONSTANTLY CONNECTED

The warm ocean breeze passed through the leaves of the palm tree, carrying with it a fresh tropical aroma. Sam had been awaiting this moment for some time now. He couldn't recall the last time he stepped away from his work to take a real vacation. Sam works as a sales manager for a medium-sized Fintech (Financial Technology) company. Over the past three years, Sam has been devoted to aiding in the growth of the organization, increasing its sales revenue by

24%. However, this has meant long hours, sleepless nights, and added stress and anxiety.

The setting couldn't have been more perfect: a private villa in the Maldives, overlooking the turquoise waters, with days of ample sunshine at an all-inclusive resort. Yet, an uneasiness lingered within Sam. "What's missing?" he thought. "Did I forget to do something before I left? Did I provide all the information my team needs to do their job?" As the anxiety started to build, Sam got up from his padded lounge chair on the water's edge and grabbed his phone, which was charging just a few meters away. Less than ten hours into his vacation, Sam was scrolling through emails, making calls, and sending texts to his team members and clients. Sam's team was perfectly capable of completing the work he had left for them in his absence. No one had dropped the ball. Things weren't falling apart. Yet Sam couldn't stop himself from jumping into work mode.

In a world where everything is at our fingertips and we are always connected, it has become more difficult to step away from our work and unplug from the busyness of life. While there is a sense of relief that comes with knowing we can easily contact someone in case of an emergency, or virtually visit people we may otherwise seldom see through video conferencing, this constant access can place high demands and stress on individuals. It can lead to us feeling "on call" all the time, and practically expected of us.

How often do you find your mind wandering from the present moment—concerned with the past or an unknown future? Like Sam, we rob ourselves from enjoying life for fear of losing control or missing out, or because we get intercepted with a host of other modern distractions.

Emotional intelligence fosters mindfulness and helps us ask ourselves: *How am I spending my time? Am I setting healthy boundaries for myself and others?* It brings awareness to and control over our compulsive urge to constantly engage, which we will discuss in more depth throughout this book.

CYBERBULLYING

My friend Molly chuckles as she recalls her first AOL Instant Messenger name—Seahorsefairy23 – back in 2004.

For a small-town girl who didn't get out much, the Internet—especially chat rooms and instant messenger—was the best creation since sliced bread. Waiting five to ten minutes for dial-up to play its jingle and log you on seemed lightning fast at the time. Especially since it was connecting you to the world! Molly and I spent hours in the evenings after school, logging on to our AOL Instant Messengers. Several of our friends would hop onto a group chat, until we were forced to log off because we were 'hoggin' the phone line.

Yes, back then it was a choice of a house phone or the Internet dominating the line.

Until then, we'd talk about the daily gossip, who's dating who, secret crushes, and weekend happenings.

This was the beginning of a revolution in the way we communicated with each other. Gone are the years where you had to wait for social gatherings, and reunions to catch up with old classmates, family, and friends. Now, you can just "follow" them on social media. Yet, with all the great wonders of the web, I don't think anyone anticipated what was to follow in the upcoming decades.

"Catfishing": Fatal Consequences

Megan, fifteen, found love in cyberspace after setting up her social media account. His name was Jake, and he claimed to be a sophomore in high school. Jake started by wooing Megan and gaining her trust. As the cyber relationship became more intimate, Megan felt comfortable enough to share her deepest, darkest secrets with Jake, and the two began exchanging suggestive dialogue. Later, Jake convinced Megan to share provocative pictures with him.

Little did Megan know that Jake was not a boy but a girl from Megan's school, Anna, with whom she'd had many confrontations in the past. Within hours of Megan sending photos to "Jake," those photos (along with intimate conversations) were broadcast across the Web.

Feeling completely devastated and humiliated, Megan could not fathom showing her face again at school. Her parents, devastated by their daughter's ridicule, decided to pull Megan from public school and home school her while they contemplated whether to move out of town to give Megan and the family a fresh start. Unfortunately, four days after the public humiliation, Megan's younger brother found her hanging by a scarf in her closet.

Megan's story is unfortunately one of many. Bullies are no longer limited to the playground or the workplace where school principals and HR departments can intervene. Instant connection to millions of people allows bullies to create mass havoc in the lives of others while also concealing their true identity if they so choose. It is estimated that over one in three people have experienced some form of cyberbullying.[5] To avoid cyber bullies, harassment, and the infamous Twitter wars, some individuals have deleted their social media accounts altogether. However, limiting our involvement on social media platforms does not ensure we are safe from being someone's emotional outlet, as we will see in upcoming examples.

Instead of nursing the symptoms of low EQ, we must start addressing the problem at its root. Megan's story is tragic, and so is the case of Anna who felt the need to bully her. We may view these perpetrators as bad or evil people, but we seldom ask, "What happened to make this individual act in the ways they did?" Could Anna have been dealing with her own insecurities, unresolved emotions, trauma, or abuse? Did Anna not have the awareness and empathy to realize how it might affect Megan? It doesn't take a villain to execute a horrific crime or inflict emotional or physical harm on others. Most terrible acts are committed by "normal" individuals, not psychopaths.

IRRATIONAL OUTRAGE AND ENTITLEMENT

At a Taco Bell in San Diego, California, two women battle it out over their place in line at the drive thru. The event was captured by a hungry customer (let's call her Denise) who was unable to get into the parking lot because the two women were blocking in parked cars and the entrance to the drive thru. Denise, who was recording the situation, got out of her vehicle after blowing her horn to try and get the two antagonists to move. Antagonist #1 says to Denise, "This is somebody cutting in front of somebody, taking advantage of the situation. No, I'm not [moving]. I'm calling the police, cause what you did was wrong, and you know it!" (pointing to Antagonist #2, who was still sitting in her car).

Antagonist #1 then got back out of her car and continued, "That's what the problem is. People ought to respect other people, you just don't... She's selfish that's, that's why her ass is overweight!" I feel it's important to add that the ladies were both around the same body type. Finally, Antagonist #2 decides to get out of her car and say her two cents, "That's the problem, she's going nuts."

Although both women were calling each other selfish and "the problem", neither of them acknowledged that their behavior was selfish to the customers who were unable to leave or get food due to their adult temper tantrum. Denise asked if either one of the women would be the bigger person and move so she could get food. Both antagonists refused. Antagonist #2 said she didn't even want food anymore but was still unwilling to move for anyone. This went on for several more minutes until the manager came out and was able to talk antagonist #1 into backing up.[6]

It's no surprise this video went viral, with millions of views. Assuming the antagonists have watched the video since the occurrence, I would be curious to know how they feel about the situation now. Do they feel foolish, or do they continue to justify their actions? Do they have any self-awareness about how their actions affected other people? What if all of us could play back moments where we lost our cool; would we still feel as strongly about our response or instead look at ourselves in horror as if we were possessed by some outside force?

These two ladies failed to display any elements of emotional intelligence. Their lack of self-awareness—reflected in their inability to see they were part of the problem; their lack of self-regulation—displayed in their inability to control their emotions; their lack of social awareness—by completely disregarding other customers' needs to get food; and their lack of empathy—for each other and for frustrated customers.

Situations like the one at the San Diego Taco Bell are happening every day across the globe. Individuals struggling with intense and irrational emotions can literally lose their ability to think clearly, sometimes leading to violent or fatal consequences.

EMOTIONAL HIJACKING: WHEN PEOPLE SNAP

Milo Brooks, a sophomore in high school at the time, was destined for success. A straight-A student his entire life and two classes ahead

17

of his age group, there seemed to be no stopping him in the pursuit of achieving his dream of attending Stanford and majoring in bioengineering. When Milo wasn't shut away in his room studying, he spent time working at the local science museum and exhibit center. Although he was shy, most of his peers and teachers found him to be a very pleasant and likable person, eager to assist in group projects and tutor his fellow classmates. On this day, however, something seemed to snap inside him.

Following final semester exams, Milo received a B- on his AP Calculus exam. Enraged (because this was the first B he had ever received) he confronted his teacher to get him to change the grade. When Mr. Johnson refused, Milo proceeded to vandalize the classroom. He flipped desks and hurled chairs through the air, aiming them directly at Mr. Johnson who ducked for cover behind his large wooden desk. With all the commotion of propelling furniture and his raging screams of "I'LL KILL YOU! I'LL KILL YOU!", it didn't take long for nearby faculty and staff to enter the room. As three of the instructors tried to talk Milo down, two other faculty ran to alert the on-site police officer.

When the on-site officer arrived, she found Milo curled up in a fetal position at the back corner of the classroom. Mr. Johnson was still hunched behind the desk in utter terror and shock at what had just unfolded. Milo's parents were notified and escorted to the station with him for questioning. When asked to recall the scene that just unfolded, Milo seemed confused, unable to remember hurling the chairs and threatening to kill Mr. Johnson. He could only recall being upset about his grade and walking to the classroom to confront his instructor. For him, the events that unfolded within the classroom were as vague and fleeting as a dream.

What happened to Milo is not an uncommon phenomenon. Often, in individuals who've experienced extreme levels of stress, trauma, or emotional arousal, the brain can suppress the recollection of the traumatic or stressful experience.

What caused such a "good kid" to lose it? Did he really intend to cause harm to Mr. Johnson? Highly unlikely. However, when in a state of furry and lacking emotional control, normal people can react with unthinkable violence as we will see in the examples that follow.

Anthony "T.J" Cunningham, who in 1996 played safety for the Seattle Seahawks, was killed by his neighbor over a feud about a parking spot. The two had agreed via text to "settle it" with a fight in a school parking lot, where T. J's neighbor pulled out a gun and shot him dead.[7]

At the AMC movie theater in Concord, North Carolina, a dispute over a seat turned violent. As William Weldon and his mother walked in, they noticed that two people were sitting in the seats they had purchased. When William showed their tickets to the couple in their seats and asked them to move, 18-year-old Bryant Eaves stood up, pulled a gun, and shot William in the leg.[8]

In Renton, Washington, a father got into an argument with his daughter about installing a baby gate for her son in the kitchen. The argument ended with Wendell Wilson shooting his daughter six times, with two of the shots direct to the head. He admitted to officers that he intended to kill her. When they asked why he pulled a gun on her, Wilson said it "comes down to a dominance thing."[9]

It is frightening to think that at any moment, time, or place, an individual—including our self—can snap. An inability to acknowledge and control our emotions should not be taken lightly. We tend to have an unrealistic view of our capabilities. While we would like to

believe we would never snap and cause harm to others, staying ignorant to the power of the mind and our emotions leaves us vulner-
able.

Most of the people who are "losing it" in this way are normal people who finally had all they could emotionally handle. We have all
had a mental breakdown at some point in our lives, even if the last
one was when we were age two and threw something at a caregiver
when we didn't get our way. As horrific as these crimes and situations are, often people are simply (and sometimes brutally) releasing
highly intense and toxic emotions that have built up inside them. And
because these people are not self-aware and do not know how to
regulate their emotions, the eventual release of their tension sends
emotional shrapnel flying toward anyone in their path.

MASS SHOOTINGS

October 1, 2017. Twenty-two thousand people gathered at the
Route 91 Harvest Festival in Las Vegas. At 9:40 PM, Jason Aldean took
to the stage as the closing act. From a corner suite on the 32nd floor
of the Mandalay Bay Resort and Casino, overlooking the concert, at
10:05 PM, a steady sputter of shots was fired. Round after round of
bullets sprayed into the dense crowd. Short pauses between rounds,
lasting from just a few seconds to a minute, allowed some to flee or
find cover between the 12 bursts of fire. Within 12 short minutes,
64-year-old Stephen Paddock fired over 900 rounds of bullets into a
sea of concert goers and law enforcement, and over 200 rounds into
the hotel hallway—the deadliest mass shooting in American history
at the time this book was written. Fifty-eight people died, and an additional 850 individuals were injured. Unfortunately, this tragedy is
one of many.[10]

Mass shootings have a long history in the United States. However, every year they are increasing in frequency and number of casualties at an alarming rate. Looking at the last 53 years as a timeframe, 50% of all mass shootings have occurred since 2000: "During the 1970s, mass shootings claimed an average of 5.7 lives per year. In the 1980s, the average rose to 14. In the 1990s it reached 21; in the 2000s, 23.5. This decade has seen a far sharper rise. As of 2019, the average was 51 deaths per year."[11] As startling as the facts are, they get even more bleak when you consider that mass shootings account for less than 1% of all gun violence in America. The other 99% is a combination of homicides and suicides.[12]

Although some might argue the individuals involved in these scenes are "psychotic or evil," This is often not the case. Mass shooters tend to have three things in common, all of which correlate to a deficit in EQ. They are:

1. Childhood trauma—affecting mental and emotional stability.
2. Interpersonal crisis or grievance— relating to relationships or communication with others.
3. Motivated by hate. Commonly led by racism, misogyny, or religious hate (which has significantly increased since 2015).[13]

Childhood trauma does not in and of itself lead to madness. It is the inability to cope with the psychological and emotional trauma that leads to problems. Toxic relationships with others, skewed perceptions, and hate are also related to a lack of awareness, emotional regulation, and empathy—all leading back to social-emotional literacy.

It's common for news media to associate mass shooters with psychiatric illness because it's a simplified way to explain this horrific behavior.[14] Yet, only a fraction of a percent of mass shooters have been identified with psychosis. This is not to say these individuals do not suffer from mental illness—but this is an extremely broad term. Close to half of the population suffers (or has suffered) from some form of mental illness—which includes anxiety and depression.

Mental illness is often misunderstood. It is seen as a chronic disorder that can only be managed by medication—which is seldom the case. We should not look at mental health any differently than physical health. If we neglect to maintain a healthy diet and exercise, we may find ourselves suffering from obesity, diabetes, or high cholesterol. Many of these health issues are a direct result of how we managed our health. If we change our habits, we have the power to reverse and likely eliminate many of these issues.

Equally, if we do not monitor our mental health, it too can lead to chronic illness. You could even argue that mental health is more important to manage than physical health. While physical illness can be fatal to the individual, the mental illness of one individual can be harmful (and even fatal) to vast numbers of individuals if not monitored and controlled.

While I believe that emotional intelligence could prevent and drastically reduce such fatal destruction, I don't want to downplay the extent of psychological aid these individuals need. It will inevitably take much more than a course on developing EQ to correct years of trauma, suppressed emotions, or firmly held prejudice. However, imagine if these perpetrators were raised by caregivers who were self-aware, could regulate their emotions—instead of taking them out on others—and were able to come from a place of understanding when interacting with people who were different than them.

Would they have experienced childhood trauma from an emotionally intelligent caregiver? No. Would this individual likely be taught how to manage conflict and their feelings in a healthy way?

Yes. Would they be raised to fear and hate others who are not like them? No.

In this way, our own EQ can determine the actions of others for years to come; what some might call the butterfly effect. Equally, who we choose to emulate and allow to influence our lives, will play a major role in how we view ourselves, others, and the world around us.

REALITY TV AND POP CULTURE: ROLE MODELS?

You may have been told as a child (or told your children), that violence never solves a problem and is not the right way to handle conflict.

However, if actions really do speak louder than words, it seems the sensory information around us (TV news, political figures, movies, and video games) portrays violence, intimidation, and screaming matches as the best ways to handle conflict.

An American Family was the first modern reality show. Airing on PBS from January to March of 1973, the show featured the Loud family of Santa Barbara, California. Pat and Bill Loud and their five teenage and young adult children (Lance, Kevin, Grant, Delilah, and Michele) volunteered to depict a "real" American family. The producers wanted to show an "attractive" family they felt other Americans could identify with, in contrast to the unrealistic comedic families depicted in scripted Hollywood shows such as *The Brady Bunch* and *Leave it to Beaver*.

During the filming of the show, Pat asks her husband Bill for a divorce from their 20-year marriage and for Bill to move out of their home, while Lance (the oldest son) announces he is gay. Although the show only aired for three months (12 episodes), it was the beginning of what we now know as reality TV that currently dominates the airwaves.[15]

Since the creation of *An American Family*, reality TV has morphed into anything but the portrayal of real life. Yet, millions of people are glued to their TV to see what drama will unfold amongst the cast. MTV set the bar for reality TV with the longest-running reality TV show in television history. *The Real World,* later changed to *Real World,* debuted in 1992 and ran through 2017. Since then, there has been an explosion of and continued exaggeration within the genre of reality TV, where cast members compete for love, money, fame, and business. Whether it's being publicly humiliated by Chef Gordon Ramsay on *Hell's Kitchen*; drama amongst toddler beauty pageant moms who live vicariously through their young daughters in *Toddlers in Tiaras* and *Pageant Moms*; or the laundry list of shows that feed on stereotypes such as *Jersey Shore, Breaking Amish,* and *Duck Dynasty*, our appetite for it does not seem to be abating. No matter what your interests, there is a reality show for you. Crafting, home improvement, plastic surgery, petting zoos, nature channels...the list goes on and on.

What makes reality TV so compelling? Dr. Jana Scrivani, a licensed clinical psychologist, believes that due to our busy schedules and increasing feeling of isolation and loneliness, reality TV fills a void by allowing us to find a sense of connection with the shows' characters and contestants. In an article titled "So, here's the science behind why we're so obsessed with watching reality shows," Arielle Tschinkel states, "It seems that the less connected you feel to people in your life, the more you may seek the drama of reality shows."[16] If that is the case, then it seems there are a lot of us who feel disconnected.

Over the years, reality TV and pop culture have continued to amplify drama, backstabbing, adult temper tantrums, screaming matches, oceans of tears (fake and real), physical brawls, and the humiliation of fellow human beings. What does that say about us viewers who drive up the ratings? Are we heartless? Have we become numb? When *American Idol* first aired, watching the auditions and the people who couldn't sing get barked at by Simon Cowell was funny and entertaining for many people. But being publicly humiliated and ridiculed may have left deep scars on contestants' self-confidence and self-worth. Some might argue that they made the choice to go on national television and make a fool of themselves, but isn't that a cop out? In the first few seasons, there were people who didn't know they were tone deaf. They thought they could sing. Does that mean we should turn their lack of talent into our entertainment?

Thanks to the media and pop culture, we are becoming desensitized to dehumanization. Our social environment today is crammed with unhealthy competition, low self-esteem, faulty communication, egocentrism, and a lack of self-awareness, empathy, and emotional regulation. We have a severe EQ deficiency on our hands.

THE PROOF IS IN THE DATA

We can't deny the facts (technically, you could deny the facts, but it would not change the fact that they are the facts); anxiety, depression, loneliness, violence, and media consumption are all on a sharp and drastic rise. And the increase in social media seems to be correlated with the extreme human behavior and epidemic of several mental disorders.

Number of people using social media platforms, 2004 to 2018

Estimates correspond to monthly active users (MAUs). Facebook, for example, measures MAUs as users that have logged in during the past 30 days. See source for more details.

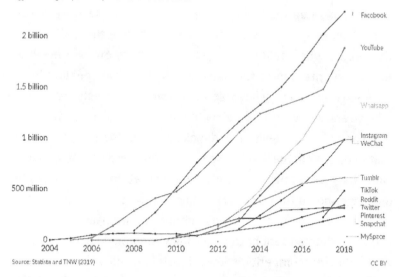

Source: Statista and TNW (2019)

CC BY

Source: Statista and TNW (2019)[17]

Number of people with anxiety disorders, World, 1990 to 2017

Number of people with an anxiety disorder, differentiated by sex. This is measured across all ages. Figures attempt to provide a true estimate (going beyond reported diagnosis) of the number of people with anxiety disorders based on medical, epidemiological data, surveys and meta-regression modelling.

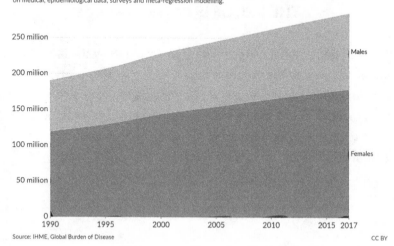

Source: IHME, Global Burden of Disease

CC BY

Source: IHME, Global Burden of Disease[18]

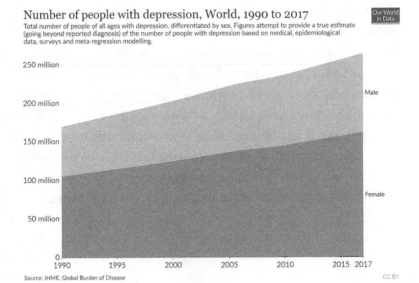

Number of people with depression, World, 1990 to 2017

Source: IHME, Global Burden of Disease[19]

THE PARADOX

If we live in a society where we have not learned how to effectively express ourselves in a way that makes us feel understood, and that our needs are being met, we are less likely to be receptive to the feelings and needs of others. The results can be frustration, anxiety, and depression, which will likely trigger a scarcity mindset, causing our system to go into survival mode. We may become defensive and hypersensitive to the statements of others. This state of mind may also lead us to misinterpret other's messages and body language and react accordingly, which then triggers the same survival mode in them. This feedback loop is what I call the EQ deficiency paradox. Once within the loop, people often want to "win" by force or intimidation which only leads to greater turmoil and consequences. The only way to escape this vicious cycle is for someone to bravely break the toxic pattern and step up to become a "superhuman", using the skills of emotional intelligence and compassion.

Unfortunately, it is hard to break out without the guidance of someone with a developed understanding of the human psyche and EQ. And while there are a number of these people out there, the ratio of high EQ to low EQ individuals is drastically off balance—currently. While most of us are aware we have a crisis on our hands, only a few know the root cause, leaving the rest of us desperately trying to find the answers and asking, who or what is to blame?

3

Eliminating Blame and Taking Responsibility

"An important decision I made was to resist playing the Blame Game. The day I realized that I am in charge of how I will approach problems in my life, that things will turn out better or worse because of me and nobody else, that was the day I knew I would be a happier and healthier person. And that was the day I knew I could truly build a life that matters."

— Steve Goodier

Eight-year-old Tommy was helping his dad repair and replace boards on the back deck. As his dad was preparing to lay down the fresh pine board, Tommy asked if he could hammer in the nail. "Sure, you can give it a go," his dad replied.

Tommy had some experience using a hammer and nails, but just to lend a helping hand, his dad held the nail steady so Tommy could focus on handling the hammer. The first drop of the hammer hit at a slight angle, just tapping the perimeter of the nail head.

"Try and bring it straight down and give it a good 'whack' to break into the wood. Then it will be easier from there," his dad assured him.

Tommy steadied his hand and with a forceful drop, smashed the hammer onto his father's hand. As Tommy's father clutched his hand in utter shock and pain, Tommy blurted out, "The hammer did it!"

Tommy's response to his father's injury points to a larger truth: In general, we are lousy at acknowledging our shortcomings and taking the blame when we deserve it. Even when we have all the data and evidence we need to prove someone or something is at fault, there will still be those who deny the cold, hard facts. And perhaps it's easy to understand why we avoid taking personal responsibility for our actions. In our political and criminal justice systems, the common practice is to dance around the allegations, deflect, or play ignorant. By using these tactics, politicians and other authority figures convey the message that it's okay to lie, cheat, and act unethically to save face and get what you want in life.

EVERYTHING IS NEUTRAL UNTIL GIVEN INTENT

To *change* how we think and behave, we must first *understand* why we think and behave as we do. This is not as simple as it may seem, as there are a multitude of factors that influence thought and behavior. These fit into two main categories: biology and environment— the classic nature versus nurture argument.

Prior to the 21st century, our influences were mainly our family, local news sources, and the commonly held beliefs of our close-knit communities. With the rise of the Internet and social media outlets in the early 2000s, our information pool has exploded. New information is literally at our fingertips; easily obtained and shared. Anything and everything can be "proven," "debunked," and debated; it's just a matter of finding the "right" information to support our preexisting beliefs—a term psychologists call confirmation bias. As we grew hungry to absorb and eager to share, information overload was born.

While data shows a significant correlation between the rise in internet usage (including social media platforms) and anxiety, outrage, depression, loneliness, and political polarization. Nevertheless, correlation does not equal causation, and although some individuals are eager to pin the blame on things such as the Internet and social media outlets, these tools are only as powerful as the people using them. The Internet and every "connector" site/app we have today would be useless and empty without us producing content and information. We are the fuel; we are the problem and the solution.

Tools are useless until we use them. How they are used determines their purpose and effectiveness. The Internet is a tool; social media is a tool. They are inherently neither good nor bad. The same goes for money, weapons, and even religion. You may have been raised to believe that money is the root of all evil. This is incorrect; money is neutral. It does not decide what it is used for or how it is distributed; people do. If we are selfish and greedy, we will likely use it to fuel our own agenda and fulfill our personal wants and needs. However, if we are a philanthropist, we may decide to use money to fund research, build community facilities, and provide for the needy.

Prior to money, bartering was used in the exchange of services and goods and, yet, there was still an upper class and lower class, greedy people and givers, rulers with lots of power and wealth and peasants who lived in poverty (and were often viewed as no more than working animals). Introducing money did not change the level of good and evil in this world. Only one common factor remains unchanged: people.

GUNS

Generally speaking, most conservative Americans and gun rights activists feel their constitutional right to bear arms is threatened due to the increase in mass shootings with handguns and assault rifles. They usually argue, "Guns don't kill people, people kill people." To a certain extent, they are correct. A gun, without a user, is a chunk of metal or plastic that has the potential to inflict harm. Meanwhile, those who are pro-gun reform want to see stricter laws to determine an individual's eligibility to obtain a gun. They also question whether assault rifles should be available to the general public at all or restricted to military use only.

As we've seen in the wave of mass shootings over the last decade, mentally unstable people are gaining access to weapons, both legally and illegally. And if we are increasingly acting on impulse (which is often the case with homicides), having a deadly weapon and pairing it with impulsive rage is a recipe for disaster.

It seems that many people are so focused on how gun restrictions will affect them that they fail to focus on the bigger picture and ask: *Why is our society facing such a sharp rise in mass shootings and gun violence in general?* Taking away guns does not fix the underlying problem: mental health. If you place people who are depressed and suicidal in a straitjacket in a padded room, you prevent them from harming themselves, but you do not "fix" or address their depression and the source of their suicidal thoughts. Similarly, when gun laws are the primary topic of conversation, the primary issue of understanding why people harm others is overlooked.

RELIGION AND POLITICS

Religion and politics are two belief systems to which many people attach their identity. In deciding a belief or party is a core part of who we are, we can prevent ourselves from being open to understanding alternative ideas, philosophies, and beliefs systems, for fear of losing our identity or being perceived as a traitor by fellow believers and group members.

Unlike guns, religion and politics are intangible, but they are just as powerful, perhaps even more powerful, due to their association with personal identity. And like other tools, whether they are "good" or "bad" all depends on how they are used. At the heart of all major world religions are shared moral principles and a focus on love, peace, compassion, and good will. Yet, over 195,035,000 people (estimate as of 2016) have been killed in the name of religion.[20] At the same time, we can argue that, through religion, thousands of hungry people have been fed, clothed, provided shelter, and saved from their bad habits due to kind hearted religious people.

Political systems also vary drastically regarding the welfare of their citizens. Switzerland and Canada for example, are ranked as two of the top global governments, providing their citizens with exceptional education, health care, low levels of pollution, and protecting their human rights and freedoms; while other nations, such as North Korea, may rule by fear, force, and manipulation, deprive their citizens of their human rights and a better life.

Why the disparity? Like many tools and systems, religion and politics are largely being abused and are often used to push personal agendas, rather than working for the greater good of humanity. In the end, we are all left with an unresolved common problem. Why does it seem so difficult for us to see both the pros and cons of either side, and thus find common ground? If we choose to justify and tolerate all behaviors and actions, simply because we feel the need to protect our religious and political views, we can create inflexible thinking, and drawing of lines in the sand – the opposite of emotional intelligence.

THE FENCE SITTER

Fence sitters are those who do not choose a side or advocate for one particular view or the other. They tend to be unfavored by many on either side of the "fence," because we like people who are like us. If we feel someone cannot choose a side, it can make us feel uncomfortable. We wonder whether they can be trusted. This is one of many maladaptive traits of humanity (which we will discuss in later chapters).

However, there are several different categories of fence sitters. There are individuals who do not take a side because they understand the complexity of reality. There are those who refuse to take a side solely because they want to avoid confrontation. Others wear different "masks" around different people to save face and avoid potential manipulation or, again, confrontation. This doesn't mean they are bad people. However, it can be very frustrating and cause us to question their honestly and loyalty.

I had a close friend of ten years who wore many faces. I believe she has a good heart but a weak backbone, for lack of a better word. She is very timid and never wants to ruffle any feathers. She also has a variety of friend groups. Around me, in reference to one of these groups, she disclosed that they were not her true friends, and she knew that they did not have her best interest at heart; but I did. She would tell me how she needed to distance herself from them and their unhealthy views and attitudes. Yet, a few days later, she would post a picture with them on social media, exclaiming how she was "so lucky" to have such "wonderful friends" and that she "couldn't live without them".

To be fair to her, she didn't have a good pool of friends to choose from. She grew up in a small town with a population of 1,636. Choices were minimal and most of these so-called friends' parents were also friends of the family. In a sense, she felt she had to get along with them. Nevertheless, this often made me wonder if she happened to be saying the same negative things about me to them. I thought of her as being more wishy-washy than a fence sitter. She wasn't unsure of her opinion or views; she just chose to flip-flop depending on the crowd or individual she was around at the time.

Some might consider me to be a fence sitter. Of course, I disagree. I too know my values and have clear boundaries and limitations regarding what I believe to be sensible and just in this world. Yet, I will always be open to learning about various perspectives and the beliefs of others. My personal moral values and beliefs transcend "sides" in that they can be held by any political or religious group as well as shared with those from diverse backgrounds and nations.

To be well-informed and truly bipartisan (not only in regard to politics), we need to understand the pros and cons that come with various beliefs, systems, policies, and arguments. If we do not, we are choosing to be ignorant to facts and different perspectives. Once we have all the information, we may decide that our initial ways of reasoning were incorrect and that we lacked the appropriate information to make an educated and well-informed decision.

Julie Irwin Zimmerman Faces a Backlash

People who have chosen to change their minds or points of view due to new information or experiences are often criticized. They're

35

called hypocrites, traitors, and weak, and they are threatened by individuals from both sides of the argument. Julie Irwin Zimmerman knows this situation all too well after the backlash she received following the publication of her article "I Failed the Covington Catholic Test" in *The Atlantic*. In her article, Julie talks about her change of perspective on the incident after watching a longer length video which provided a broader account of the situation, unlike the initial two-minute video Julie saw on Twitter the day prior.

The two-minute clip showed a confrontation between students of Covington Catholic High School and Native Americans from the Indigenous Peoples March near the Lincoln Memorial. Julie states in her article: "[The video clip] made me cringe, and the smirking kid in particular got to me: His smugness, radiating from under that red MAGA [Make America Great Again] hat, was everything I wanted my teenagers not to be."

According to Julie, in the initial clip, which she viewed on Twitter, Julie observed the students "menacing a man much older than them" and chanting, "Build the wall!" She also recalls watching as the "smirking kid" blocked the path of Nathan Phillips, the 64-year-old Native American elder who was playing the drum and chanting in front of a small group of high school students.

Julie wasn't the only one to be taken aback by this video. The footage was broadcast on almost every major and local news channel, newspaper, and social media outlet. It went viral. The students of Covington Catholic High School (even those students who were not in Washington, D.C. at the time) were threatened and harassed—which in and of itself depicts yet another deficiency of EQ.

On Sunday (the day after Julie watched the clip on Twitter), a new, longer video emerged, showing events prior to the high school students' encounter with Phillips. A crowd was hurling insults and nasty remarks at the Covington Catholic High School students. What originally seemed to be the students blocking Phillips' path was actually Phillips approaching the boy. In Phillips' words, he (Phillips) was trying to "diffuse the situation." Although the video still shows the students appearing to laugh and mock the Native Americans by moving their arms to mimic tomahawk chops, it offers a much different perspective than the first video clip does.

Julie states, "I did find a confrontation more complicated than I'd first believed."

To Julie's point. If we want the truth, we must search beyond the bites of information being presented to us. A sign of high EQ is the ability to feel comfortable saying, "I don't know enough about this situation to make a judgment, nor to have a strong opinion", instead of defending a side you believe to be the truth with very little evidence.

She goes on to talk about how we seem to get so involved and outraged over situations we know little about. We make judgments based on the vague evidence that is presented to us without seeing the situation in its entirety. It was difficult for Julie to admit she may have been wrong about her initial take on the situation. In an *NPR* interview on the *Hidden Brain* podcast, she said, "I was afraid to tell a few people, initially, that I had changed my mind...which is crazy! Why can't you just say, you know, 'I think I was wrong about this,' but I knew some people would be upset because it's as though you are giving your enemy ammunition by admitting that they might be right and you might have been wrong. And you can't ever show weakness or admit that maybe the other side has a point." [21]

Demonstrating high EQ isn't easy. And, as Julie experienced, even when we step up and take responsibility for our misjudgments, we can still be vilified for our actions. We (the collective society) often say we admire and respect people who can admit when they are wrong; who look at the facts; are open-minded and humble. However, what it seems we are saying is: You can do all these things as long as it supports what I believe to be the truth. Otherwise, you're spreading lies and "fake news."

The belief that someone is only worthy and credible if they stand with us, is yet another indication we lack emotional intelligence.

How often do we find ourselves defending something or someone simply because they identify, at some level, as a member of our tribe? We seem to gravitate to ideas and situations as being black or white, failing to recognize that we are living in a world of grey. Sorting through vast amounts of data is draining and time-consuming and, in a demanding world, we tend to settle for headlines and default to agreeing with our side because doing so is easy—not necessarily because it's right.

If we want to see a more compassionate, productive, happier, healthier, and prosperous world, we must stop assigning blame and start accepting responsibility. We all know it wasn't "the hammer" that did it.

THE COMMON FACTOR

As I said earlier, we (the people) are always the common factor. The things we blame for society's lack of civility and deep thought (the Internet, social media, religion, politics) are only the tools we use to support and propagate our beliefs and opinions. However, while we are the problem, we are also the solution. It's the choices we make and the actions we take that send messages of either understanding and compassion or condemnation and hate.

However, to become a catalyst for a revolution in human awareness and to harness the power of our minds, we must first undo the indoctrination of social norms and our biological evolution toward conformity and primal reaction. We will look at this in more depth through the upcoming chapters.

"We are the creative force of our life, and through our own deci-sions rather than our conditions, if we carefully learn to do things, we can accomplish those goals."

—Stephen Covey

4

Governance and Indoctrination

"As a species we're fundamentally insane. Put more than two of us in a room, we pick sides and start dreaming up reasons to kill one another. Why do you think we invented politics and religion?"
— **Stephen King**

A society is destined to fail without some form of order. Without structure, our world would be a ball of chaos.

Human government has taken many forms over the centuries, from tribes and clans led by chiefs and elders, to the democratic republics of the ancient Greeks and Romans, from monarchies to communist parties and authoritarianism, and finally to the democracies of today's First World countries. No matter how different these structures of government are, they all have a common goal: to establish some form of law, order, and control.

Throughout history, various forms of consequence and punishment have been enforced to deter us from committing crimes and to encourage us to act in the best interest of society. Punishment can take many forms: a monetary fine, public humiliation, jail time, or more brutal forms of physical punishment, even execution. For most of history, the fear of punishment has been largely effective, but not everyone fears the consequences of human law, especially if their chances of getting caught are very low.

Only in recent decades have advancements in science and technology allowed us to solve once unsolvable crimes. Forensics, digital surveillance, and DNA analysis are new in the grand scope of human civilization. If our ancestor's crimes and self-serving agendas were more likely to be overlooked, unsolved, and unpunished, what other factors may have deterred them from free-riding, cheating, breaking laws, and committing minor or heinous crimes? Religion—specifically religions who believe in punitive gods—have been shown to serve as a deterrent to crimes that once may have gone unpunished.[22]

In the upcoming sections, we will look at both the benefits of religion to human behavior, and how governance and indoctrination of any kind—with stated guidelines, rules, and expectations—may cause some people to act in accordance with the law—of man or of a higher being—for fear of punishment or eternal damnation.

RELIGION: A CULTURAL INNOVATION?

The major world religions (Islam, Christianity, Buddhism, Judaism, and Hinduism) have only existed for the past 5000 years or so. This is not to say that other religions did not exist beforehand. Rather, religion as we have come to know it, with its complex and elaborate rituals, powerful gods, and vast numbers of followers, has only been around for a short period of human history.

Coincidently, these major world religions were born around the same time human civilization began to expand. We no longer lived in tribes of around 50-150 people. Instead, we were living in cities with thousands of individuals.

A popular anthropological theory is that without god-fearing religions, complex modern societies may not have come into existence as we know them today. The belief in a punitive, all-knowing god reinforced the law of the land and thus allowed large societies to function.

Individuals not only faced worldly consequences if they were caught committing a crime or doing something "bad", but also feared the punishment that awaited them in the afterlife.

Supporting this theory is the fact many of today's smaller cultures (tribes, clans) seem to have a distinct structure when it comes to rule, order, and religion. If these close-knit societies do have religion, their god or gods tend to look quite different from those of the major world religions. Rather than providing a moralistic and punitive function, their gods tend to be "tricksters"—playful, less powerful—who are much less involved or concerned with the lives and well-being of humans.

How does community size impact our tendency to commit crime? When our ancestors lived in smaller groups where they knew most and perhaps even everyone, they were more likely to weigh the costs and benefits of cheating, stealing, or adultery. Getting caught could very well mean life or death, along with the risk of being ostracized or banished from the group (which might also lead to death). At the very least, it may have cast a negative light on the perpetrators and their families. Thus, would-be criminals may have felt more motivated to restrain themselves from acting on emotional impulse. In contrast, if our early ancestors had lived in societies of thousands (or millions) of people, then committing a crime against a single individual may not have been perceived as having as severe an impact on the group. In that case, a punitive god would have kept their behavior and actions in check.

This belief in a moralistic and punitive god is key to understanding human motivation and behavior. Societies and individuals who believe their god to be benevolent and forgiving are more likely to cheat, lie, and steal according to multiple empirical studies. For example, anthropologist Benjamin Purzycki has noted, "Moralistic, punitive, and omniscient deities appear to push cooperation and fairness beyond one's local in-group."[23] Let's look at Purzycki's research in more detail.

Purzycki and his team selected 591 religious' participants from eight different societies around the globe. Their subjects included horticulturalists, hunter-gatherers, business owners, and wage laborers. The study was meant to test altruism among strangers who were members of co-religious groups (members of the same religion). Each participant was given a six-sided die (with each side depicting one of two colors), two cups, and a stack of coins. The rules of the game were simple. If the die landed on a side with the color "a," they put a coin in their own cup. If the die landed on a side with the color "b,", they put a coin in the cup that would go to an anonymous co-religious stranger. At the end of the game, all participants could keep the coins they had accumulated.

The participants—although given rules—could cheat with impunity. The results suggested that participants who cheated and favored self-interest over a regard for strangers correlated with how much they feared a punitive god. Participants were questioned about their gods only after taking part in the game.

The findings were significant; fearful believers gave five times more to co-religious strangers than those who believed in a more benevolent (forgiving/loving) god. The latter were more likely to cheat and keep the coins for themselves. Was the fear of a supernatural punisher the glue that encouraged moral behavior?

CULTURAL GLUE

As said before, all major religions arose as civilizations became increasingly large and complex, particularly during times of scarcity or hardship, religion taught and encouraged cooperation when it was desperately needed. Naturally, us humans are hesitant to trust those whom we do not know well, seeing them as outsiders. Because our species spent thousands of years cooperating in small groups of 50-150 people, we tend to trust only those within our inner circle or in-group. With the expansion of modern civilization, limiting trust to solely our in-group posed a problem when it came to collaboration and trade with strangers—that is, until today's major world religions came along. These religions offered a shared set of values, beliefs, and sacrifices that connected us far beyond our political systems and national borders. Such value systems, along with the shared belief in an all-knowing, moralistic god, was an important element in the growth and effectiveness of large trade networks and diplomacy. Regardless of nationality or personal connection, a shared belief was enough for strangers to establish trust. Without some form of religion, we may not have flourished into the modern human civilization we are today.

THE CONSEQUENCES

Religions, governments, and societies revolve around a set of rules and expectations, some of which we are taught not to question. As members of societies, we are expected to abide by the laws that have been set forth. There is a downside, however. Social and religious rules can create complacency and diminish individual thought and creativity—a key component to self-awareness and open-mindedness.

During the early stages of our lives, our choices are limited. We have no choice in what we eat or how much, what we wear, where we live, the parents we're born to, the environment in which we are raised, and our race, nationality, or religion (or lack thereof). At the same time, religious beliefs and social norms are established at a young age and, as we grow up, we tend to accept them as our personal beliefs and truths as well as part of our identity. We may be admonished when we question it, asked to stop asking so many questions, and instead encouraged to follow "the script"; to have faith and loyalty. These commitments to institutions and cultural groups encourage us to defend things we may not fully understand.

The weaving of religious and cultural beliefs into our social DNA may explain why we can encounter strong, negative emotions and defensiveness when we challenge another's beliefs—and why we may have the same response when our own beliefs are questioned. We tend to view questioning and challenge as a personal attack.

Emotional intelligence allows us to see beyond belief systems (of any kind), past scripts, and past the fear of punishment. It transcends our differences and alienating labels and allows us to compassionately feel a variety of emotions. If we feel bitter, instead of lashing out or punishing ourselves for feeling bitterness, we ask, *"Why do I feel bitter?"* and address the source of the feeling. When we are angry, we do not hold our tongue because it is deemed "wrong" by God or society, we hold our tongue because we understand the deeper reasons behind our feelings and address it appropriately, understanding the ramifications of our actions on the other person.

To be clear, it is not to say an individual can't be religious and have high EQ. You can have both. Emotional intelligence simply extends beyond a system of beliefs, meaning an individual can be an honest, empathetic, compassionate, open-minded, and trustworthy without governance of man or religion.

BECAUSE, I SAID SO

When children ask questions or challenge authority, they often hear similar responses: "It just is!"; "Because I said so!"; "Stop asking so many questions!" These responses deter a child from being curious and may create the belief that questioning is disrespectful and rebellious. Who dares question an authority figure? Thus, by the time we are adults, we are more likely to accept, without question, what we have been told is true, right, wrong, and culturally acceptable.

We often forget (if we were ever aware at all) that everything we have known to be true from a young age was indoctrination. We have been taught how to behave, what we believe, the words we use and the meaning we assign to things. This lack of awareness makes it difficult for us to detach ourselves from these conditioned beliefs and prejudices. However, once we are able to separate our true self from the conditioned components of our life, we can approach conversations regarding topics such as religion, politics, and other hot topics with an open mind, considering numerous perspectives. That experience can be absolutely beautiful and enlightening. Until we do so, we will continue to follow the scripts set forth by society.

In the upcoming chapter, we will observe several scenarios which compare conditioned behavior (automatic reaction) to mindful behavior (carefully considered)—demonstrating the qualities and benefits of high EQ.

5

Be Polite. Know Your Place.

"In politeness, as in many other things connected with the formation of character, people in general begin outside, when they should begin inside; instead of beginning with the heart, and trusting that to form the manners, they begin with the manners, and trust the heart to change influences. The golden rule contains the very life and soul of politeness."

— Lydia Maria Child, *The Mother's Book*

Behaving "appropriately" correlates to likability and cooperation. Etiquette, the customary code of polite behavior in society, or among members of a particular profession or group, varies from culture to culture. We enact these rote greetings and behaviors, day in and day out. Yet, how many of us ask ourselves: *Why do we do what we do and say what we say? Who decides what anything means? Why do I need to say I'm sorry if I am not? Why are we polite?*

Most of what we know about manners is another form of conditioning. You may recall from childhood, or have recently witnessed a parent (maybe yourself) reinforcing polite and culturally acceptable responses and behaviors. For example:

"What do you say?" – Encourages the child to respond in a way deemed appropriate i.e. "Please." and "Thank you."

"We don't do that." – Labels the behavior as unacceptable.

"That's not nice." or *"That was nice."* – Points to what is considered good behavior or bad behavior.

"Don't do that." "Stop that." "Go do____." – Commands to restrict and shape behavior.

"You are being too loud."
"You need to tone it down."
"You have too much energy."
"You need to sit still."
– Judgmental statements that point out inappropriate actions.

"If you do ___, then ___ will happen." – Threat of consequence; potential scare tactics.

These statements are commonplace in our society today. Some people do not have an issue with them. In fact, they may argue that by not enforcing expectations, creating structure, or setting boundaries, they will not be good parents and instead will create hellions, brats, and miscreants. However, commands, threats, and dead-end punishments will never solve the root cause of misbehavior. They are only a temporary deterrent.

Guidance and structure do not need to be eliminated from parenting. However, there are more effective ways to get long-term results. Currently, most of us teach our children what to do and what not to do, and how they should or should not feel. It's no wonder that, as adults, we find it difficult to express and control our emotions. Telling others what they should do and how they should feel leads to a lack of introspection, self-awareness, regulation, empathy, and genuine understanding. These crucial abilities are being over-looked and dismissed in parenting—likely unintentionally— resulting in a deficiency of EQ. If we want to set our children up for social-emotional success, it is crucial to provide them with opportunities to think, feel, and express themselves in a healthy and authentic way. Imagine the positive results if we were taught why and how to come from a place of compassion and understanding versus being told what we "should" do.

Let's look at two different responses to the same event. The first reflects a traditional parenting style, using reinforcement of socially acceptable behavior and norms, while the second dives a bit deeper into understanding the child's emotions.

SCENARIO ONE:
(TRADITIONAL PARENTING)

Jacob, age three, and his dad are at a Little League baseball game where Jacob's older brother is playing. Jacob is fidgeting on the bleachers and play-ing with a baseball his dad gave him. A group of young kids (around Ja-cob's age, maybe slightly older) are playing catch close to the bleach-ers. Jacob's dad, noticing his restlessness, suggests that Jacob "go play with his friends." Reluctantly, Jacob eases his way down each bleacher, step-by-step, pausing near the bottom and glancing back at his dad. "Go on. Have fun."

Seeming disappointed in his dad's reply, Jacob descends the rest of the way down the bleachers. Holding the baseball tightly against his chest with both hands, Jacob makes his way to the outskirts of the circle of children, again glancing back at his dad, who gives a nod of reassurance and a smile.

A few of the children notice Jacob's presence and rush over to him. Within minutes, a shrill cry comes from one of the children, grabbing

Jacob's dad's attention. Jacob's face is scrunched up with a scowl and narrow brows, his body turned slightly away from the group while he tightly clutches his baseball.

Now both Jacob's dad and the parent of the crying child are at the scene.

Jacob's dad: (with a look of concern and disappointment on his face) Jacob, what happened?

Crying child: (being consoled by the parent) He pushed me!

Jacob's dad: (addressing Jacob) Jacob, why did you push her?

Jacob: She tried to take my baseball.

Crying child: Nu uh! We asked if we could play with it and he pushed me.

Jacob's dad: Jacob. That wasn't nice. We don't push people. What do you say?

Jacob: (mumbling under his breath) Sorry.

Jacob's dad: She didn't hear you. Say it like you mean it.

Jacob: (louder) Sorry.

Jacob's dad: That's better. Now give her a hug and share your baseball with them. It's nice to share.

Jacob: (gives a hug but is reluctant to share, groans)

Jacob's dad: If you can't share, I will have to take the baseball away. Do you want me to take your baseball away?

Jacob: NO!

Jacob's dad: Then share and play nicely.

Parent of crying child: (*seeming satisfied with the discipline meted out by Jacob's dad, and addressing his daughter*) Take it easy, don't be too aggressive.

○   ○   ○

Jacob's dad's response seemed to resolve the issue—or did it? The underlying feelings, resulting in the cause and effect, were never addressed. Reinforcing social norms and expectations does not actually change anything deep within us. It simply smooths over hard feelings without encouraging us to feel true remorse or to accept responsibility. Group norms don't meet and validate our emotional needs. Is it any wonder that many of us experience so much anxiety, depression, judgment, gossip, and drama?

Now let's take a look at a similar situation and apply emotionally intelligent parenting.

SCENARIO TWO: (EQ PARENTING)	*Jacob, age three, and his dad are at a Little League baseball game where Jacob's older brother is playing. Jacob is fidgeting on the bleachers and playing with a baseball his dad gave him. A group of young kids are playing catch*

close to the bleachers. Jacob's dad, noticing his restlessness, asks if he is interested in playing with the other children. Reluctantly, Jacob shrugs his shoulders.

Jacob's dad: (*trying to verbalize Jacob's body language*) Are you feeling worried or uncertain about playing with the other children?

Jacob: *(nods in confirmation)*

Jacob's dad: What specifically are you worried about?

Jacob: *(shrugs shoulders)*

Jacob's dad: *(trying to find the source of concern)* Are you worried they won't like you?

Jacob: No.

Jacob's dad: *(searching for clues, noticing the baseball is clutched tightly in Jacob's hands)* Are you afraid they will take your baseball?

Jacob: *(nods in confirmation)*

Jacob's dad: If you knew they would not take your baseball, would you want to play with the group?

Jacob: *(nods in confirmation)*

Jacob's dad: What if we went over and talked to them and let them know your concerns. Would that be okay?

Jacob: *(shrugs his shoulders)*

Jacob's dad: *(patiently)* Well, it sounds like we have a few options. One, we can sit here and watch your brother play. Two, you can go play with the kids, but they may try to take your ball if you don't tell them what you're feeling. Or three, I can go with you to talk to them and we can decide from there.

Jacob: Talk to them.

Jacob's dad walks with him to the group of kids, allowing Jacob to make the first move by asking to play with them. Then Jacob's dad drops down on one knee to position himself at eye level with the other children.

Jacob's dad: Jacob would love to play with you all, but he wants to tell you what he is feeling first.

Jacob: (*holding tightly to his baseball*) I don't want you to take my ball.

Jacob's dad: (*restating his son's concerns*) Jacob is worried that you might take his baseball. Can we agree not to take Jacob's ball? (*addressing Jacob*) What if they play with the ball, but promise to give it back? Would that be okay?

Jacob: (*nods in confirmation*)

Jacob's dad: Sounds like a plan. I'm going to leave you to play now. I will be at the bleachers if you need anything. Okay?

Jacob: (*with a slight smile across his face*) Okay.

Both scenarios end with Jacob playing with the other children. However, in *scenario one,* Jacob's needs were not met, which led to a confrontation, a forced apology, and an expectation that Jacob should get along and share with the other children (not by Jacob's choice). In contrast, in *scenario two,* Jacob's feelings and needs were understood and met. With some help from his father, he was able to express them, and the other children also affirmed his needs, eliminating possible upset and confrontation. Jacob was willing to share and play nicely with the other children but, this time, by choice.

Some naysayers will disagree with the strategy recommended in *scenario two*. Let's examine some of the potential criticisms.

"You're teaching our children to be soft!"

Do you mean that teaching children how to understand and express their emotions is "soft"? Then yes, that's exactly what I am recommending. However, I dislike the word *soft* because understanding and expressing emotions in the appropriate way is extremely difficult. Doing so requires lots of energy, self-awareness, empathy, humility, and the strength not to fall victim to our primitive urge to react. In other words, emotional intelligence. Cavemen fought with fists and sticks, but we are not cavemen and we shouldn't want to be. We are advanced, intelligent *homo sapiens*. Perhaps our greatest power comes from our ability to understand and control our emotions, giving us the ability to successfully convey and interpret messages, address our needs, and better understand and support the needs of others.

"Kids shouldn't control the situation. We are the adults here!"

Those who utter such a statement likely heard it from their own parents or other adults when they were helpless children who were not given the opportunity to express their needs or emotions. Thus, they are continuing the cycle.

We are not relinquishing our rights or control as a parent or authority figure by listening to and understanding our child's feelings. Instead, we are empowering them to own their emotions and learn

54

how to properly identify and articulate their feelings and needs, which few adults today know how to do.

> "It takes too long! I don't have time for all of that dialogue."

Finally, the infamous excuse: I don't have time. The conversation in *scenario two* did take a bit more time and thought. However, I would argue the extra time and consideration was well worth the outcome. And not just the outcome of this one situation. This way of thinking becomes habit and helps us to develop these critical skills early in life. Ultimately, this skill-building will save us countless hours in the future by avoiding miscommunication and the resulting headache, heartache, and stress. Emotional intelligence allows us to thrive as leaders and foster healthy relationships.

Saying we don't have the time is nothing less than an excuse. If we make the time to watch our favorite shows, hang out with friends, and tinker around the house on nonessential projects, then we have the time to develop a fundamental and life-altering skill. The only thing that may hold some of us back is (1) our will to devote time to something that isn't always easy, and (2) allowing our ego to hold us back. As the saying goes, many things worth having aren't easy to acquire.

TAKING THE TIME MAKES A DIFFERENCE

These exact words—"I don't have the time!"—were uttered after I took the time to de-escalate an argument between the gentleman who made this statement and a panelist at a conference. This attendee had taken extreme offense at what the panelist said, and he made sure to tell her why she was "wrong," and to claim that his interpretation of what she said was correct.

Once the panelist had all she could take and saw she was getting nowhere with this man, she simply walked away, leaving his rage ungrounded and his needs unmet. I decided to seize the moment, seeing it as an opportunity to satisfy this man's emotional needs to be understood. As I spoke with the gentleman for a good 20 minutes, I made sure to:

- Listen to his underlying emotional needs (the message behind the words)
- Satisfy his need to be understood and heard.
- Continue open dialogue.

The conversation continued something like this:

Me: How do you feel about the conversation we are having?

Man: Good. But you're not the one who said all those things. So, I'm not upset with you.

Me: Yes, you're right. I didn't say those things. However, I never said that I agreed with you. I only said that I understand how you might have interpreted what she said as a personal attack.

I merely took the time to listen to you. What if, instead of approaching her with anger and attacking her remarks, you approached her by expressing how what she said made you feel, why it made you feel that way, and then gave her an opportunity to empathize and explain her intent? In this way, you are giving her the benefit of the doubt. Do you think the conversation would have ended as it did—unresolved, with both parties feeling upset, stressed, and unheard?

Man: No. But nobody has time to talk feelings all day long. I've got other things I need to do with my time.

Me: I hear what you're saying. It does take some time. However, I witnessed you argue for over five minutes with this woman before she walked away from the conversation. How long would you have continued to argue if she hadn't stepped away? The approach you took led to a more time-consuming interaction. With respect, sir, I don't feel it's necessarily about the amount of time it takes to listen and understand, as much as it is the amount of energy and control one has to possess. Would you agree?

Man: I suppose, but that just isn't reality.

Me: And who determines reality?

We determine the reality in which we experience and interact with life. We can all come up with excuses for why we do not put more effort into our behavior and actions, but at the end of the day, if it is important to us and we see the value, we will find the time to devote to altering our mindset and communication.

Changing our construct from *what* to *why* makes a huge psychological, behavioral, and emotional difference. Being told *what* to say is nothing more than a conditioned and reflexive command. For generations we have been programmed with scripts that run in the background and that take up little bandwidth of cognition. We regurgitate and react as instructed, which requires us to have little (if any) genuine connection to what we are saying, or to the circumstances and the feelings of those around us.

PUTTING <u>WHY</u> BACK INTO OUR VOCABULARY

If you have been around a young child long enough, you likely realize that "Why?" is in their top ten word choices. And, once you answer that initial question of "Why", it is likely to be followed with another, and another, and another, until you have dug as deep as your knowledge on the subject will allow.

By answering their "why", we are fostering growth and development and engaging children to form a hypothesis to answer their own question. We are developing their problem-solving skills and boosting their (earned) self-confidence and creativity. With all these benefits, why do so many whys go unanswered?

As stated earlier, I am a people watcher; fascinated with human behavior, communication, and engagement. There are so many things we can learn from simply observing, and there are times when simply observing can be difficult.

I find it's important to understand how seemingly subtle remarks and actions can have long-lasting impacts on the human psyche; especially during the early years of one's life. Distinct lines are drawn, and certain behaviors are either encouraged or discouraged. This is the age where the "why" thrives or is smoothed. Remember, "It's not polite to ask too many questions". But why?

Are we simply impatient people who don't want to take the time to develop a child's self-confidence, knowledge, and creativity? Of course not. The more likely explanations are:

- We are unaware that ignoring or condemning this three-letter word can have long-lasting impacts on how we communicate, problem-solve, and perform into adulthood.
- We are simply reinforcing our own parents' parenting style: "My parents did XYZ and I turned out just fine."

This is not to suggest that dismissing your children's "why" will cause them to spend the rest of their life in a therapist's office. However, there is a much higher likelihood they will struggle with assertiveness and confidence, and refrain from sharing their ideas for fear of judgment or dismissal.

Some readers may be hesitant to change the way they view politeness and structure their childrearing (which is clearly their right). However, it is worth stressing that just because something is the "norm" doesn't mean there isn't a more effective and engaging approach. We can easily get mentally stuck on the idea that if we are "normal," then all is well. But what if normal isn't all it's cracked up to be? What if there is a better way?

THE CONSEQUENCES OF NOT QUESTIONING AUTHORITY

Questioning an authority figure seems taboo in many cultures, even in the autonomous culture of America. But what exactly defines authority figures? Is it the simple fact they are older than we are? According to this definition, a teenage camp counselor is an authority figure to a younger child. Do teenagers, who are still learning and developing, have the ability to give orders? In this context, yes.

Often, authority figures are highly educated (especially those who carry letters before or after their name: Dr., MD, PhD); they manage or lead others; or, are subject matter experts in their field. Mostly, though, how we define and assess authority figures is very subjective. In many cases, we define authority largely on how we perceive ourselves in comparison to others in a specific hierarchy. If I work as a laborer, my authority figure may be my supervisor. Although my supervisor has no formal education beyond a high school diploma, she has experience in the field and a title that implies she is someone I should respect and defer to. Yet my supervisor may be considered inferior to someone with many more years of experience, a college education or higher title.

Our view of ourselves also plays a major role in how we view the authority of others, including the question of whether it is appropriate to address or question them. For example, in the military it is considered highly disrespectful to question or challenge a higher-ranking person in the chain of command. Moving up within the chain of command takes hard work and earned merit. Even in civilian life, while we are not definitively held to such expectations, there is often an unspoken rule to "know your place."

Succumbing to authority is a primal instinct that spans most of the animal kingdom, where survival of the fittest, and respecting and submitting to the alpha, are the norm. If a creature dares to challenge an elder or alpha of the group, it should be well prepared for a bloody fight, possibly to the death. Like our ancestors, we may suffer physical defeat, and we can also face social exile, which could be just as damaging to our well-being and survival.

In short, the feeling we get in the pit of our stomach that stops us from speaking up and questioning authority is essentially ingrained in us; it reveals our natural fear of exile, and other negative consequences. I can't assure you that, if you speak up, you won't face scrutiny. What I can promise you is, if done right, respectfully, assertively, and compassionately, others will notice, and that display of higher EQ will earn you respect and potentially provoke great change.

While I am not asking that you start a large movement, I do want to show that ordinary people, who express themselves and their beliefs and needs appropriately, have single-handedly made change. For example, Rosa Parks, an African American women who sparked a movement for human rights when she refused to give up her seat on a bus in 1955; Todd Beamer, and other passengers on Flight 93, who took control of the plane hijacked by a 9/11 terrorist; Lilly Ledbetter, who fights for equal pay; Malala Yousafzai, who campaigns for better education for women, and the list goes on. There is a long history of extraordinary individuals who escaped the gravitational pull of instinct and employed not only high EQ, but courage, strength, and sacrificial acts for the greater good of humanity.

CORPORATE HIERARCHY

In the workplace, CEOs and other executives can seem far out of reach to many within their organization. Some employees even view them as celebrities. The distance created by rank and accessibility may prevent us from speaking up about important issues; we worry that our input may fall on deaf ears or, worse, result in negative consequences for questioning our superiors. Other employees may idolize these high-ranking individuals, overlooking their errors and poor decisions.

This hierarchy of power, and authority figures' ability to intimidate and punish, poses a serious threat to not only the organization but also the individual employees. We can't place all of the blame on the people at the top. It is every employee and stakeholder's right and responsibility to speak up, even if speaking up simply means asking, "Is this weekly meeting really a good use of our time?"

Having worked with founders and senior level executives for several years now, I can tell you they are normal people with normal people problems. I can also tell you that their success rarely comes from having superior intellect. More often it is the result of putting in long hours and hard work. However, there will always be those who move up in a company by way of skilled manipulation (organizational politics).

The point being, we should not be intimidated by someone's title. We all have blind spots, even leaders, and none of us are good at everything (not even close).

Great leaders are not afraid of having their actions and behaviors questioned. In fact, a confident leader–an emotionally intelligent leader–encourages it. They understand that these insights can lead to further development of their personal and professional success. It is those who are not confident in themselves and are afraid to "lose face" that scoff at being questioned.

Be wary of those who use micromanagement, years of experience, and bottlenecking to keep others in check. These individuals tend to be the first and last to speak and are often eager to criticize or pin blame on others, thus endangering the health of the organization. I have often found that those who make us fear speaking up are often the ones who we need to question most of all.

FATAL OBEDIENCE

Medical errors are the third leading cause of death in the United States. An estimated 250,000 individuals lose their lives every year at the hands of those whose job it is to save lives, not to take them. These errors include mistakes made by incompetent staff, misdiagnosis, dosage mix-ups, errors of judgment in care, and system defects (computer or medical equipment malfunctions). While some of these circumstances, such as equipment malfunctions, are beyond our control, most of these deaths are due to human error caused by overwork and understaffing.[24]

Having family members and friends who work as nurses, pharmacy technicians, and pharmacists, I can say that some of the circumstances these professionals are put in would cause the best of us to fall prey to error. While getting my blood drawn at a lab, I noticed that the professional was also answering the phone, checking people in, and setting up the lab all by herself. When I questioned the lack of staff, she said, "This is normal for us here".

The company usually only had one or two staff always present. She mentioned being concerned for her safety, being all alone. That, if anything were to happen, there would be no one else around to help. In clinics and hospitals (in the US), staff frequently report they are expected to take on more responsibility and work longer hours which can lead to mental fatigue and burnout. I want to address this poor working environment because I feel it is important not to pin the blame for error on one cause. For the purpose of this chapter, we will be focused on how perceived authority affects someone's willingness to be assertive as well as the weight that someone's opinion carries, based on rank.

Some of these fatal errors result from arrogance at the top. Arrogance directly correlates with low EQ, where self/social-awareness, empathy and self-regulation are often absent. For example, Theresa Brown, a hospice nurse and a writer for the *New York Times*, notes that doctors have been trained to believe: "They're the person who speaks. They have all the responsibility. The buck stops with them, but it also means they don't really need to listen to the nurses."[25] In other words, Brown implies that all doctors are trained to think of themselves as superior to nurses.

Clearly, not all doctors believe that their title alone makes them superior to nurses. Nonetheless, numerous studies have shown that authority (and where we see ourselves in the social hierarchy) play a major role in how we communicate and interact with one another. If a nurse feels intimated by a doctor, they may be less inclined to challenge a diagnosis or questionable prescription. By simply donning a white lab coat, an individual is likely to earn our respect and credibility, regardless of their actual credentials. They are less likely to be challenged and more likely to have their orders followed.

One of the most cited and controversial studies of the twentieth century was conducted in the 1960s by Yale University psychologist Stanley Milgram. Milgram wanted to determine the extent to which a person would go in delivering deadly electric shock when being instructed to do so by an authority figure (in this case, someone wearing a lab coat). The participants in the study were labeled "teachers", and their role was to ask questions to the "learners" (actors in the experiment who were instructed to frequently reply with the wrong answer). When the "learner" responded with the incorrect answer, the "teacher" (participant) was expected to deliver an electric shock. These shocks—which, unbeknownst to the participant, weren't real—ranged from 30 volts (mild shock) to 450 volts (lethal shock). With each wrong answer, the "teacher" was instructed by the experimenter in the lab coat to increase the voltage. As the wrong answers accumulated and the shocks reached dangerous levels (which was reflected by the audible screams of the actor playing the role of the "learner"), a few of the participants became hesitant to continue administering the shocks. However, after persistent instruction to continue by the experimenter in the lab coat, 65% of participants knowingly proceeded to administer the maximum voltage of 450 volts (a lethal shock); and all participants administered shocks of 300 volts.[26]

The moral of the story is this: We need to be careful how we define and idolize authority. Our view of authority is learned, not innate. As a child, I always assumed adults had all the answers, because that was implied. Many children are taught to respect their elders because they are "wiser." However, many adults are immature and irresponsible; age does not automatically confer competence or wisdom.

Should we be teaching our children to trust and respect simply based on seniority and power, or should we teach them to respect others while *also* feeling empowered to step up when they believe an action or behavior needs to be challenged or questioned?

What I am suggesting can easily be misconstrued. I am not dismissing the value of expert opinion. Equally, I don't think we should overrule someone's hard-earned knowledge only because we disagree, or that we should look to disprove it using flimsy information from search engines. High EQ encourages respect *and* healthy debate. When we simply argue for the sake of proving our point, and begin to dismiss authority figures who are well-informed, we are only adding to the deficit of EQ, not promoting it. However, it is appropriate to speak up when we recognize an error, and to ask ourselves: *Is this person credible? Are they acting ethically?*

WHEN "CHALLENGING" AUTHORITY PROVED BENEFICIAL

Three months prior to graduation, Rebecca was offered a job working with an industry-leading Fortune 500 company. After the interview, she left feeling discouraged. What she was told would be a behavioral interview seemed more along the lines of a technical interview. The position was in technology (her minor), and the questions seemed to be heavily focused on application software, types of languages, and her experience with programming projects. With five leaders in the room playing round robin with interview questions, Rebecca felt her body start to tense with every new question thrown at her. As the interview ended, they asked, "Is there anything more you would like to tell us about yourself?"

At that point, Rebecca would have bet everything that she had lost her chance at getting this job, and when you feel you have nothing left to lose, you sometimes give it all you have. Prior to the interview, Rebecca had done her research on the company, part of which was reading its entire 28-page vision and values statement. At that moment, one thing stuck out to her and she said, "You know, this entire time you have asked how much I know about this position without really knowing what I can bring to this company. Yet, your vision and values statement says, 'We don't care how much you know until we know how much you care.' Would you like to know the value I plan to bring to your company?"

Rebecca notes, "I think I literally saw a jaw drop from the gentleman across the table, and every eyebrow in the room raise. I left the interview and immediately headed to my Java professor's office (who, prior to the interview, was talking highly of me to the internal recruiters who arranged the interview). 'I blew it. It was terrible!' I said. 'I told them that computer science was my minor, but they continued to throw technical questions at me!' He reassured me that everything would be fine, regardless of whether I got the position or not. And followed by asking how long until I would know if I got the job. I told him a week or two. They have a few more days of interviews left."

The next day, Rebecca found it difficult to focus on her coursework. All she could think about was what a fool she had made of herself in front of five senior leaders of a Fortune 500 company that she really wanted to work for.

Rebecca recalls sitting in her three-hour psych practicum, about to present on her research, when her phone started to vibrate. "I would usually let it go to voicemail, but my gut said to answer it."

Her professor was kind enough to let her step away to take the call. It was one of the internal recruiters from the interview the day before. "Clearly, they were calling to put me out of my misery, instead of making me wait a week to tell me I didn't get the job, which I appreciated." She said.

The recruiter asked Rebecca, how she felt the interview went.

"I thought, *Lady! Stop pouring salt on the wound!*"

"It was awful!" Rebecca replied.

She told the recruiter she had felt ill-prepared because she thought the questions were going to be behavioral when they turned out to be mostly technical.

The recruiter apologized for the confusion and then quickly interjected. She told Rebecca the reason for her call was to extend an offer for the position.

"After picking my jaw up off the floor, I accepted the offer! I thought what the hell just happened!?"

A few months into the position, Rebecca asked her hiring manager why she had been selected. "She told me it was my last statement. The fact I was bold enough to address how they conducted the interview and then proceeded to back my case with a direct quote from their vision and values statement."

Rebecca was told what she did took "guts", and it showed she had what it takes to lead and spark change.

The point of the story? It takes courage and confidence to assert yourself but, more importantly, emotional intelligence to do it in a way that is respectful and objective.

"I'm proud of myself," Rebecca said. "The old Rebecca, the less confident, emotionally unstable Rebecca, would more than likely have broken into tears from failure to answer their questions. The old Rebecca would not have done research on the company in advance. I got the job because my actions stood out, respectfully."

There is a fine line between confidence and arrogance, assertiveness, and aggressiveness. Rebecca, though upset that the interview wasn't what she expected, was able to acknowledge her frustration and approach the situation objectively. She displayed control over her emotions, and was able to communicate how she felt effectively, demonstrating emotional intelligence—which proved highly effective. Not only did Rebecca gain the position she earnestly wanted, she also gained respect from senior leaders.

If we want to see change, whether in our society, government, or institutions, we must acknowledge our personal fears and understand their origins, to question ideologies and methodologies with emotional intelligence. We must realize our fear of authority is only as real as we allow it to be. It's important to realize that being genuine and assertive does not mean we cannot still be respectful and polite. This process of getting comfortable with finding our voice takes time, effort, and getting out of our comfort zone. It's not easy, and there are no shortcuts or quick fixes. Ultimately, however, it is for our own good and the greater good of humanity.

6

Everybody Wants a Quick Fix

"Real change happens bit by bit. It takes great effort to become effortless at anything. There are no quick fixes."

— **Geneen Roth**

Life hacks, as they are called, are great ways to shave time off our daily tasks, organize our lives better, and simplify chores. Tired of having to pull every cleaning product out from under your sink to find the one you need? Easy peasy! Use a clear hanging shoe rack (placed on the back of your utility closet door) to create ease of access, quick visibility, and better organization of your cleaning products. Quick and simple.

Unfortunately, not everything in life can be "hacked," despite the promise of marketing taglines such as "Five easy steps to achieving the perfect body!"; "Ten steps to a happier life"; and "The seven habits of a more productive team!"

As applications, devices, and services that automate and supposedly simplify life proliferate, it seems that we should be able to manage every aspect of our existence—our relationships, behaviors, moods, jobs, and weight—with a quick "how to" guide or an app that does most of the work for us. This desire for the quick fix explains why we feel disappointed when we try a diet for a week and don't see the results we expected, or we try meditating a few times and don't find inner peace and clarity instantly. This failure to achieve the desired results can quickly lead us to feel that things "just are" and can't be changed, causing us to throw in the towel. The feeling of helplessness that is likely to arise with unrealistic expectations can lead us to chronic anxiety, stress, and depression. To develop our EQ, we need to understand that any type of improvement, or the achievement of any goal, is a long-term process that requires work and dedication.

HOW-TO GUIDES AND WORKSHOPS DON'T CREATE ALL-STARS

Coach Leach's high school basketball team was ready to make a comeback from a brutal previous season. Today was a special day for Leach and his team. The high school was able to bring in former NBA player, Steve Roberts[1], to speak to the team about strategy and co-operation on the court. Roberts shared key learning experiences he had accumulated throughout his 18-season career, which he found invaluable in playing and interacting with his teammates. Roberts also reviewed and critiqued footage from several of the high school team's games, addressing what the team did well and possible areas for improvement.

After Roberts's presentation, Leach gave a final pep talk to the team before beginning the evening's practice. Straight away, Leach observed as the team seemed to immediately begin applying a few of the cooperation techniques Roberts had just outlined. He was looking forward to seeing this same energy in that week's big game.

To Leach's disappointment, his team lost—terribly. What happened? Why didn't the team apply the strategies and the techniques suggested by Roberts? Why did they fail to successfully cooperate with one another?

---

[1] Steve Roberts is a fictitious character in place of an NBA player.

The reason is simple: How-to guides and workshops don't create all-stars. There is a big difference between knowing something and applying it in the real world. If I told you that a motivational and informative speech from a professional athlete would take your mediocre team to the championship finals, you would probably say, "That's absurd," and rightfully so. We can't expect information to create transformation in and of itself. It takes practice, repetition, a change in mindset, and fine-tuning to develop a set of skills. Similarly, changing how we think, behave, and react with more emotional intelligence requires patience and skill-building.

Some organizations deny that emotional intelligence is all it's cracked up to be: "We tried that stuff and it didn't work. It's just a bunch of fluff." But what specifically did they try, and for how long? Nine times out of ten, the organization brought in a single speaker or conducted a lone workshop, retreat, or team-building activity. The remaining 10% probably took the form of longer programs that could have been effective but lacked organizational commitment. Perhaps leadership failed to buy in to the program by not investing enough time, effort, or a positive mindset. The inevitable result is failure.

The point is simple: We don't expect a high school basketball team to transform into an NBA basketball team overnight, so why do we expect such rapid results of ourselves and others? That is simply not how our brains operate.

WE ARE NOT COMPUTERS

Our brains are often compared to a computer. Yet, our brains operate in ways that are vastly different. Computers process information far more quickly and are far superior to us in terms of their computational and problem-solving abilities. Within seconds or minutes, they can calculate information and crack codes that would take even the most intelligent of humans several lifetimes to solve. It only takes a quick upload of code to run a program and get an answer.

In contrast, we are much slower learners. Classical conditioning and the adoption of social norms, in a sense, are forms of "programming." These "scripts" guide our day-to-day lives without our having to think about them. But these programs were not uploaded overnight. Instead, it took years of reinforcement, trial and error, and mirroring of others to form what is now a set of unconscious responses, beliefs, and habits.

When we assume our problems can be resolved with a one-off application, or some new information, we will be met with disappointment.

QUICK FIX EQUALS QUICK FAILURE

As long as there is a deficit in EQ, there will be organizations and individuals who use workarounds and aggressive strategies to display "successful" results. Why? Because quick fixes appeal to our emotions and a desire for instant gratification. While cheating or heavily concentrated efforts may produce quick results, the long-term effects are usually negative. For example, you may lose weight quickly on an extreme diet, but this also comes at a cost. Studies show that, if you reached your weight-loss goal through a crash diet, you are more likely to gain your weight back, and perhaps even additional weight, for several reasons.

First, depriving yourself of the things you love takes discipline, which requires energy. You may have found your productivity was negatively affected; you may have had less tolerance for the people around you; and you may have noticed a change in your mood from fending off cravings and fighting hunger pains. Once you reach your goal, you are eager to once again enjoy life: "What is one scoop of ice cream? I deserve it. I worked hard, and I can easily lose it again." You gain weight, and so you begin dieting again. This cycle of on-again, off-again slimming is called yo-yo dieting, and its results are not sustainable.

Second, your body doesn't realize you are dieting and may assume you are starving. Thus, whatever food you are consuming that isn't being burned off is being carefully stored as fat. You also begin to burn muscle as well as fat (which accounts for some of your weight loss), and the result can be a significant impact on your metabolic functions.

The point is that quick results aren't a healthy or sustainable approach to weight loss—or any desired change.

The same is true for any long-term goal. If we do not get out of this mindset that there is a quick fix for everything in life, we will be severely disappointed, time and time again. Even our natural abilities—such as athletic or artistic ability—need training and refining. And for us to be great or exceptional, we need discipline and continuous practice.

"Overnight successes" do not often occur overnight in reality. They were years in the making, and we do not see the challenges and the many failed efforts that took place before success happened. We see only what appears to be instant success. Ask anyone who has accomplished greatness in life and what it took to get to where they are today. Few of them will say they found their success quickly or easily.

But what if it's not about mastery? There are individuals and organizations that see developing skills—often soft skills—as something to check off the list. A great example of this quick fix attitude is compliance training.

☑ CHECK IT AND DONE

To comply with laws and meet regulation requirements, organizations must offer this training. It's a necessary evil for them, yet it still doesn't prevent things from going wrong. A 2018 *Training Industry* report stated the average midsize business spent (on average) $2.1 million on compliance training, while the average large organization spent nearly $20 million. In the United States alone, approximately $87.6 billion is spent annually in compliance training.[27] Yet, according to a 2013 Gallup report, an estimated $450-$550 billion is lost every year (in the United States alone) due to hidden problems within organizations related directly to employees and leadership.[28] In other words, the cost to organizations of training people not to screw up, combined with the cost of screwing up, is roughly $537.6 to $637.6 billion in the United States every year.

What is the point of training if it is an expense without positive results? Compliance training, if done right, has been shown to reduce the cost of settlements, damages, and fines by 37%.[29] Unfortunately, many organizations ignore its full potential and view it as just another item to check off their to-do list.

APPEARANCE ISN'T EVERYTHING

It seems we have lost our appreciation for true mastery of a skill. Instead, we want things fast, right now, and the market has provided us with exactly what we've asked for. For example, there are many master classes and "certifications" that insinuate you are a subject matter expert within mere hours or weeks of completion. While mostly offering good information, these types of trainings and certifications provide little more than surface level knowledge on subjects.

I'm not saying you shouldn't continue to learn or take these courses, but we must see them as they really are. If we really want to educate ourselves, increase our performance, and improve our overall well-being, we need to change the way we measure real success—not through one off certifications that look nice on our wall or on a resume, and remain dormant in our brains. We need to fundamentally change our process and mindset to achieve our desired results.

We must become aware and avoid the lure of a bargain and a quick fix. Most of the services and resources that promise a solution to our problems will likely fall short. When it comes to EQ, a "Five steps to becoming more emotionally intelligent" guide is not going to deliver. Yet, even the best of us can be drawn in to a quick and simple solution. Why is it that even those of us who are aware of these ploys still fall victim to their enticing fantasy?

We may not want to hear this but, by nature, we humans are very irrational beings and lead first with our emotions—how things make us feel. In the upcoming chapters, we will take a deeper look at the mechanics of the human mind, what makes us tick, and how to override innate ways of thinking and behaving.

PART 2

WHAT MAKES US TICK?

7

Designer Flaw

"Does the human being reason? No; he thinks, muses, reflects, but does not reason ... that is, in the two things which are the peculiar domain of the heart, not the mind, politics and religion. He doesn't want to know the other side. He wants arguments and statistics for his own side, and nothing more."

— Mark Twain

Many of us who have spent time scrolling through social media feeds and watching or listening to news reporters, sports commentators, or bickering politicians may conclude that humility and simple human kindness are rare. Yet, studies show that we long for genuine human connection, gravitate toward humble leaders, and collectively feel extremely anxious with the current state of our society. What are we missing? Why do we seem to thrive on and feed the very behavior and conflict we disapprove of? The short answer is that human behavior complex.

Our world is not perfect, and neither are human beings. Yet, when our beliefs or actions are questioned, we often rush to defend ourselves, because we often struggle to accept the fact that we might be wrong. Why does it seem—as a species—we are constantly contradicting ourselves?

In this chapter, we will take a deep dive into understanding how our biological instinct to stay alive can interfere with our efforts to develop emotional intelligence.

SURVIVAL IS KEY

The key driver of all living creatures is survival. What survival entails varies from creature to creature, aside from basic needs such as food, water, and the proper environment. Survival to our ancestors meant they had to be one or more of the following: strong, dominant, healthy (absence of disease, ability to procreate), intelligent (quick-witted, crafty), or, potentially most important of all, part of a group with these strengths (safety in numbers). The speed at which our ancestors could assess a threat quickly and act also determined their likelihood of survival. There was no time to stare at a saber tooth tiger and contemplate if it wanted to play while it ran toward you and your family. You may not have lived to finish that thought.

Many of the behaviors we exhibit today derive from a combination of nature and nurture. In other words, we're born with fears and instincts that were passed down through human evolution (nature), but many of the things we perceive as threats come from conditioning and experience (nurture). It is important to understand how this combination of nature and nurture has led to the current EQ deficiency and how we can better manage it, thus increasing our emotional intelligence.

Through the process of natural selection, nature often improves itself, eliminating the behaviors and traits that do not seem to work and continuing those that do. However, this natural survival of the fittest has been disrupted in humanity. Thanks to advances in science and technology, we can cure diseases that would have killed many, and we have developed a system of laws for those who are not strong enough to protect and fend for themselves.

Considered in the context of the entirety of human evolution, the laws and systems that protect us are new. This is why we are still hardwired to defend ourselves at the first sign of threat and why we rely more heavily on impulse and emotion than rational thinking. Also hardwired into our DNA is our desire to be part of a group or tribe.

Unfortunately, some of these characteristics that we once relied on for our survival are becoming more of a threat to the survival of humanity. The collective term for this set of outdated behaviors, impulses, and ways of thinking is maladaptive. It describes a failure to adjust adequately or appropriately to the new environment or situation.

MALADAPTATIONS

In his book, *The Story of the Human Body: Evolution, Health, and Disease*, Daniel E. Lieberman discusses the many physical maladaptive traits of homo sapiens. This includes lower back pain (from walking upright), flat feet, and the desire for foods rich in calories (carbohydrates, sugar, and fats) which helped us to survive in times of scarcity. The latter perfectly exemplifies how maladaptive traits (if not managed) can sabotage us, and lead to obesity in an era of food abundance and increasingly sedentary lifestyles. However, in this book, we are concerned only with psychological, social, and behavioral maladaptation. These evolutionary behaviors and ways of thinking heavily impact how we react to, navigate, and interpret the world around us.

Becoming aware of, understanding, and controlling these behaviors is key to increasing our EQ and evolving humanity into more emotionally intelligent, compassionate, and collaborative beings.

These innate ways of behaving and thinking are not all bad. There is a reason why they are still present in our biological construct today. However, the ways in which we live and interact with one another have drastically changed. Humanity has seen more social and technological evolution in the past 50 years than some of our ancestors experienced over the span of hundreds of thousands of years. And, because most of us are unaware of the innate ways in which we think and behave, we are also unaware of their significant impact in terms of the challenges we are facing today. By bringing these maladaptations to light, we now have the choice to use our amazingly powerful and plastic (malleable) brains to catch up with our current state of being.

Let's now take a look at the innate behaviors and traits that can hold us back from evolving into more emotionally intelligent beings.

BIAS

When most of us think of bias, we typically think about the implicit (unconscious) or explicit (conscious) bias and prejudices that are associated with negative feelings, stereotypes, and discrimination against individuals who belong to or identify with a certain group. Racism, sexism, homophobia, nationalism, and religious prejudices tend to be associated with negative bias.

These same stereotypes can also be associated with positive bias. Positive bias means you may think more favorably of certain groups, have the tendency to overestimate a positive outcome, and/or put more trust or certainty in a person or group's abilities. For example, we may feel a positive bias toward our loved ones (our children and partners) and our sports teams. However, even a positive bias can have negative outcomes.

If we choose to blindly follow individuals or groups we trust, just because we favor them or agree with most of what they say, we can allow ourselves to be taken advantage of; they can use that trust to propagate a self-serving agenda masked as support for the welfare of humanity.

Being a teacher for a few years, I developed a good eye for assessing whether a child was average, delayed, or gifted, based on academic and developmental standards. Every child has something to offer, regardless of where they stack up in the eyes of the educational system. However, I found that most parents believed their child was superior to peers. Most of these children were good at what they did but, nonetheless, average. Parents were eager to label their children as geniuses if they could count and recite the alphabet, not realizing that most children their age have also developed rote memorization.

If we have an unrealistic perspective of our children's abilities and intelligence, we may find ourselves setting unrealistic expectations that they are unable to reach due to a skill or aptitude barrier. When a child is told they are naturally gifted, smart, a genius, or extraordinary in any field, they may be inclined to put in less effort. When they then do not get the results they expected, this can be highly frustrating for them. For parents, having an unrealistic perception of your child's abilities can equally cause frustration and upset when they don't perform at the level you believe they can. Instead, you may see your child as lazy, wasting their talents. This is not to say there aren't gifted and extremely talented children in this world, there are, but the majority of parents who believe their child is one of them are mistaken and displaying a positive bias.

Sports teams, arguably a close second to family when it comes to allegiance for some people, are often the recipients of positive bias too. No one wants to think of their team or themselves as "the loser." If a team had a bad season, most devoted fans will say, "Next year, we'll make a comeback." Same goes for the likelihood of winning a game. Although the consequences of positive bias may not always be as destructive as the behavior and actions that accompany negative bias, they still skew reality and can leave one feeling let down, disappointed, and ashamed. Other individuals may simply justify or deny the facts to prevent themselves from acknowledging their bias—leading to an EQ deficit.

Often, we may not even be aware of all the biases we hold. These are called implicit or unconscious biases. And, oddly enough, these biases may be completely counter to what we believe to be true or fair. The following riddle is a good example:

A father and son are in a horrible car crash that kills the dad. The son is rushed to the hospital. Just as he's about to go under the knife, the surgeon says, "I can't operate—that boy is my son!"

For many people, the riddle is a conundrum: "This question makes no sense. The dad died in the crash." Here, the implicit bias is the assumption that the surgeon was male. Even if you believe men and women are equally capable of the job, our environment often depicts certain individuals holding certain positions or exhibiting certain behaviors. Regardless of whether we are aware of a stereotype or generalization, our subconscious may direct us to these assumptions—even if we do not stand behind them—as is the case with many who read this riddle. Implicit bias impacts people every day, from whether we get a call back for an interview, to our approachability, subjective worth, or trustworthiness.

Assessing Your Own Biases

In 1995, Anthony Greenwald (University of Washington), Mahzarin Banaji (Harvard University), and Brian Nosek (University of Virginia) developed the IAT, or Implicit Association Test to understand unconscious attitudes and biases. When taking the test, subjects are given words and pictures to sort into various categories. The speed at which the items are sorted reflects how closely they associate the given concepts. Quicker sorting means a stronger association. For example, you may be shown a picture of a male (on the left of the computer screen) and a female (on the right of the computer screen). You are then asked to sort words associated with caregiving on the right (under the picture of the woman) and words associated with careers on the left (under the picture of the man). As the words appear, you must click a key to sort the words into their proper category. The next task may ask you to switch the career and caregiving column, while the computer leaves the image of the male and female in their original positions. If you take longer when sorting the career terms (now on the right with the female image) and the caregiving terms (now on the left with the male image), you may have an implicit bias in terms of roles and responsibilities in regards to gender. I took this test for the first time while obtaining my degree in psychology. The results were unsettling.

Stereotype vs. Generalization

It's important to understand how stereotypes, generalizations, and bias influence how we make sense of the world around us. Although some people use the words *stereotypes* and *generalizations* interchangeably, their definitions are quite different. Merriam-Webster defines *generalization* as:

: a general statement, law, principle, or proposition

: the act or process whereby a learned response is made to a stimulus similar to but not identical with the conditioned stimulus.

A *stereotype* is:

: something conforming to a fixed or general pattern
especially a standardized mental picture that is held in common by members of a group and that represents an oversimplified opinion, prejudiced attitude, or uncritical judgment.

To put it simply, and in the terms of Alan Headbloom from *Feel Like You Belong*, "Generalizations are helpful, and stereotypes are hurtful."[30]

Here are some example of generalizations. An apple could be generalized as fruit. A grizzly bear could be generalized either as a bear, an animal, or a mammal.

Here are some examples of stereotypes. All police officers are prejudiced against Black people. All Asians are good at math.

Both generalizations and stereotypes make broad statements about groups. However, while generalizations try to sort by similarities and make sense of the world, stereotypes tend to anchor negative judgments to a particular group. We cannot help but generalize. They help us quickly identify if someone or something is a threat, thus allowing us to assess the world around us with minimal brain power, compared to mentally dissecting every possibility. However, if we are not careful, our generalizations can turn into stereotypes.

Attitudes

Attitudes play a major role in deciding if a bias is positive or negative. Following the terrorist attacks of September 11, 2001, many people developed negative attitudes towards members of the Muslim community and to anyone who appeared to be of Middle Eastern descent. Women who wore hijabs (headscarves), and men with turbans and long beards, were viciously attacked, threatened, and harassed by strangers. One Muslim woman shared with me the horrifying story of her and her two young children almost being run over in a grocery store parking lot while walking back to their car. The attacker steered their car straight toward the family while yelling out the car window, "Go to hell, you terrorist!" The driver barely missed the targeted victims as the mother and her two children darted between two parked cars. The Muslim woman explained that, prior to 9/11, she had never feared for her family's safety or felt they were viewed as outcasts in their community.

The attitudes we have toward people, places, and things are directly related to our personal experiences or the impression made by second and third-party sources.

Seeing is Believing

Prior to moving from her small town of Albion, NY to inner-city New York, Rachel viewed it as a place where it was not safe to walk the streets at night, a place where you were very likely to get shot, mugged, or raped, and a place that offered few outdoor activities.

Aside from a concert and an event at the Convention Center (neither of which had made a negative impression), Rachel had no experience of New York. Her attitude toward the city was purely based on what she'd been told by her grandfather and hometown locals, and how it was portrayed on the local news. It wasn't until Rachel began dating someone who lived in the city that she began to experience it firsthand, which changed her attitude and perception. Rachel said, "I came to realize that others' impressions of New York were very skewed. Sadly, if I hadn't experienced New York for myself, my negative bias toward the city would likely have stayed the same." Going home to visit, many people who knew Rachel had moved to New York would say, "I could never live in the city. I like to enjoy the outdoors too much." Others expressed their concerns over safety, and some talked about overpopulation. Yet, none of them had spent enough time (or anytime) in New York to experience what it had to offer.

Like Rachel prior to moving to New York, and her friends and neighbors, without having awareness of the reality that exists beyond our personal opinions, bits of information we observe in the media, and the limited perspective of others, we are not fully able to grasp the truth. And while we can never know everything there is to know, EQ allows us to be aware of our ignorance and emboldens us to question information that is portrayed as absolute and factual.

OPINIONS AND JUDGMENTS

The next time you listen to a news channel, sports commentator, or as you scroll through social media, take the time to notice how many of us speak in absolutes: "You are an idiot!" "This is a disgrace to our nation!" "I have the most amazing husband/wife on Earth!" "___ is the best athlete to have ever played ___."

There is nothing wrong with having an opinion. In fact, there is no way to avoid having them. Regardless of what our opinions may be, we should not expect everyone to share our opinions.

As much as I would like to say I do not fall into the trap of judging others who are not like me, this is an area I have to monitor carefully and consciously redirect my implicit bias—so as not to add to the EQ deficit.

When we see someone acting or presenting themselves in a way that, in our opinion, is inappropriate, or often unconventional, we may find ourselves quick to judge them.

Developing emotional intelligence doesn't mean you will cease to judge others or have ill feelings or thoughts about them. It does mean that you will be aware of when you are making a judgment, understand where that judgment stems from, and correct and redirect your thoughts and behavior, allowing you to be more curious, open-minded, and accepting of differences.

While opinions (beliefs, theories) are not fact, they are often stated as such. Although most of the time they are innocent and do no harm (e.g., "Chocolate is the best flavor of ice cream"), other opinions, when stated as fact, can create great conflict and tension if they challenge a strongly held belief. For example, one might say, "Any man who feels it's appropriate to wear skinny jeans is gay." I use this derogatory statement to make a point that this opinion, masked as fact, not only amounts to a biased and inaccurate judgment, but can create extreme hostility and intense emotions.

When we are in conversation or internal dialogue runs through our head about something or someone, we should be careful and examine our choice of words. Are we stating our opinion as exactly that, an opinion, or are we stating our opinion as fact and therefore making a judgment?

How to State an Opinion (Not as a Fact):

In my opinion ...
I believe ...
I think ...
Personally, I ...

Some may dismiss the importance of packaging our thoughts and feelings in a way that increases our EQ, stating they don't want to feel the need to always be politically correct. However, ensuring we are careful not to turn our opinions into fact is more than being respectful to others. It also increases our own awareness that our statement is our belief, and not the gospel truth.

Activity: Catching Opinions Stated as Absolute Truths

Tune in and listen to your favorite talk show, news channel, sports commentator, or as you scroll through social media. As you listen or read take note—tallying is great to keep track—and notice how many times they speak or write in absolutes. It doesn't matter whether you agree with their statement—sometimes you do, other times you don't—it's all about paying attention to *how* it was stated.

On a few occasions, I still manage to catch myself making a remark as though it's fact. When I do, I vocally make the correction. For example: "Video gaming is a waste of time. Correction, I personally believe video gaming is a waste of time." This not only reminds me to be careful of how I present my message, it also shows to others involved in the conversation, that (1) I am aware I turned my opinion into an absolute statement, and (2) I can openly correct it and admit when I am wrong. My hope is to lead by example, showing others how rephrasing our messages makes a difference, and that it's okay to admit we are wrong and make corrections. I encourage you to give this a go. Take note of how you develop a keen eye for identifying opinions addressed as fact. More importantly, how you correct yourself for using such absolutes.

TRIBALISM

The feeling of instant connection (possibly excitement) when you encounter a perfect stranger wearing a t-shirt with your college mascot on it is a perfect example of in-group bias: the tendency to favor one's own group, its members, its characteristics, and its products.[31]

A few summers ago, my husband and I travelled to Italy. While we were waiting for the train to take us from the Cinque Terre to Montepulciano (a small rural town located on the outskirts of Tuscany), we noticed two college-aged women with backpacks, speaking English, and sitting on the adjacent bench near us. The fact they were speaking English wasn't what got my attention; it was their accent. A familiar American southern drawl. When the train arrived, we all hopped on. The two ladies sat directly across from us. A few minutes into our ride, I couldn't help but interrupt their casual conversation and ask where they were from. What were the odds? We lived just 30-miles from one another! Prior to realizing we were practically neighbors, I instantly took an unexplainable liking to them, based purely on their accent. When I found out we lived close to one another, that liking was only amplified. It was as though I had run into long-lost friends. Yet, if I had been on a local train, back in the States, with these same ladies, there is a particularly good chance I would have never sparked a conversation with them or felt even the slightest connection.

Many studies have attempted to explain how and why we have such an unexplainable connection to people we don't know, and how geography and context can influence the intensity of the connection. That connection occurs when we meet someone who appears to be part of our in-group or tribe.

Feeling connected and being part of a group can be extremely rewarding and beneficial, allowing us to develop our social networks. Indeed, early humans developed this trait to increase their chances of survival; being part of a tribe was a matter of life or death for our ancestors. Tribes offered protection and greater defenses against predators or enemies. They also offered access to greater material resources. You didn't have to be good at everything, because everyone had a role to play. However, a lot has changed in the past 10,000–12,000 years.

But what exactly is tribalism as we experience it today? And how might a lack of awareness about it negatively affect the well-being and cooperation of humanity?

Tribalism is a pattern of attitudes and behaviors we tend to adopt when we come to identify with our tribe(s).[32] Tribalism is just one of many adaptive strategies that functions and benefits us at an individual level; our loyalty is rewarded with the material and emotional support we need to survive and flourish.

Although tribalism may benefit us at an individual level, it can have a negative impact on how we operate as a society. Extreme tribalism can lead to polarization that makes it impossible to work toward a common goal. For example, the extreme political polarization we are seeing in recent years, across the globe, is bringing us dangerously close to becoming a dysfunctional society.

Tribalism begins at home. At a young age, we begin to adopt the beliefs and values of the people we are around the most, likely our closest of kin. For example, if your family is religious, you are likely to adopt their religious beliefs without question. You will also start to build a set of moral principles that determine your stance on topics or issues, such as corporal punishment and abortion. These views then bind you to other individuals who share these beliefs, creating an in-group that extends well beyond the family circle.

Many people belong to more than one tribe. For example, the members of your religious affiliation comprise one tribe, while those who share your political affiliation comprise another.

While identifying with a tribe is natural and can be very comforting, it can also create a false sense of separation and belonging that dissuades us from cooperating with members of our out-groups, those people who (we choose to believe) do not belong to our specific in-group. We may also form an inflated positive bias toward the people in our in-group; dangerously hinging on their every word without question and defending or justifying their inappropriate behavior—which we would condemn if enacted by a member of the out-group.

The size of our in-groups can vary drastically, from just two members to billions of individuals. The criteria we use to define groups is extremely broad and includes:

- Nationality
- Sports team affiliations
- Socioeconomic status
- Diverse-ability
- Political affiliation
- Support of laws/rights
- Hometown
- Religion
- Age
- Sexuality
- Hobbies
- Education
- Career field
- Beliefs

—the list goes on and on. Two people could both identify with the same group when it comes to career fields but identify with a different tribe when it comes to morals. Because moral views are stronger, they tend to outweigh the preference for the common career field. Thus, in this case, the two individuals have some commonalities but are less likely to feel connected to each other.

THE DANGERS OF TRIBALISM

Humans share a variety of common values, feelings, and needs. But when we allow our differences to get in our way, we suffer in the long run.

Kevin deLaplante has several videos on YouTube that explain tribalism. In his video, "The Dangers of Tribalism," he explains that "tribalism can lead to serious social and political problems." With lower levels of polarization, there is more tolerance for disagreement, and we recognize that we may have more similarities than differences.

With increasing polarization, the extent and amount by which we disagree makes it difficult to respect one another and find common ground. At this level of polarization, we tend to see "the others" as being completely irrational.

In-group solidarity feeds on out-group animosity, which can lead to the worst in humanity: dehumanizing the outgroup; committing hate crimes; prejudices; racism; bigotry; violence; genocide. And, if we have institutions to prevent violence, we are still left with a public culture where our in-group, out-group relationships are dominated by suspicion, hostility, and fear.

"Another casualty of polarization is epistemic: when we cut ourselves off from other points of view and only look to our tribe for guidance on what to believe and who to trust. We run the risk of erecting a system of beliefs that is increasingly unmoored from that of reality. We can see everyone that is outside of that epistemic bubble as a liar, untrustworthy, unmoral ..."[33]

HOW WE SEARCH FOR AND LEGITIMIZE TRUTH

Although we may feel a connection to certain people, and prefer them over others, we probably aren't always aware of the source of our feelings. That is, we often think, feel, and behave in ways that run at a subconscious level. If we had to rationalize every decision, we would use enormous amounts of energy and time, and limit our productivity, laboring over cost-benefit analyses.

For that reason, we rely heavily on how things make us feel, default to social norms and conditioned beliefs and values that have been ingrained in us, or defer to a trusted source, typically an authority figure of our in-group. Our group identity is a strong predictor of how we feel about particular situations or issues. When we restrict ourselves to this way of decision making, thinking, or feeling, we are leaving a lot on the table.

An important way to develop our EQ is to take the time to question the origin and validity of our beliefs, values, and the social norms we enact on a day-to-day basis. In doing so, we will likely find that most of the information we consume has come from sources we trust. Based on that information, we form what we think is an educated opinion on the matter. But, without doing that research, we can't validate that the information we're consuming is the whole truth. A popular saying, "there are two sides to every story," should be a reminder that the facts seek the validity of various perspectives. A "good" scientist is said to try to disprove their own theory, because it's only when they cannot disprove any longer, that they know they are on to something. Unfortunately, many people do the opposite and seek out information to confirm what they already believe to be true. Similarly, we tend to ignore or avoid information that might challenge our thinking. Let's use Santa Claus as an example.

If I am a child whose classmate has just said to me, "Santa is not real; your parents are really Santa Claus," I may not be ready to accept there is no Santa. On top of not wanting to accept there is no Santa, I may also believe that I have enough evidence to prove Santa does exist. In addition, my in-group believes Santa exists. So, I build my case to defend my belief:

- Mom and Dad told me Santa is real, and they don't lie. Plus, they told me stories of when Santa visited them when they were children.
- A lot of other children believe in Santa. They have many stories to share about their experiences. Some even claim to have seen him—providing testimony to his existence.
- I write letters to Santa every year. I put a stamp on them like any other real letter and I mail it to the North Pole address. If Santa isn't real, then how would I be able to mail a letter to the North Pole?
- I "know" that my letter must get to Santa because, on Christmas morning, many of the things on my list are under the Christmas tree. The fact that specific things I asked for were under the tree on Christmas morning must mean Santa is real.
- If Santa isn't real, how do you explain the presents appearing overnight? I watched Mom and Dad go to bed, so they couldn't have put them under the tree.
- There are books, songs, and pictures of Santa everywhere dating back to well before I was born. Therefore, he must be real.

My argument is clearly 100% in favor of proving the existence of Santa versus disproving the existence of Santa. When I present this evidence to the opposing party, my classmate may say:

- I know Santa is not real because my parents told me he was not real.
- If Santa is real and he does magically travel all around the world delivering presents to all good children, why do some children in other countries not know about Santa? And why do some children not receive any toys?
- I once gave my parents a letter to mail to Santa but secretly wrote another letter that I mailed at school. I asked Santa to ignore the first letter (with a different list of toys) and to bring me what was on my second list. Yet, on Christmas morning, the only toys under the tree were from the first list. Therefore, he must not be real, and my parents were truly Santa all along.
- Last, if Santa has a "Naughty or Nice" list, and only the nice children are supposed to get presents, then why do a lot of mean bullies at school get cool toys from Santa? Either Santa isn't real, or he is a liar.

In such debates, both parties often feel the other is being irrational and ignorant.

Once we have established a viewpoint, it can be exceedingly difficult to alter it. Only those who search for the truth objectively can look at both sides of the argument without bias, and fully weigh the pros and cons, looking at information and research from reputable sources. Searching for objective information must begin with the question: "What are we truly in search of, the facts or what we *want* to be the facts?"

If you answered, "the facts," how can we seek out credible information? Here are a few tips for sifting through fact versus biased or fictitious information, and half-truths:

1. **Take Nothing at Face Value**

    We should be wary of all forms of media outlets to ensure they provide us with well-rounded and unbiased information. The media makes money by "selling" us on catchy and exciting headlines—and there is more competition than ever to win our attention.

    While they may provide snippets of the truth, these outlets do not have the time or the resources to deliver the whole truth. While the "information gatherers" may be experts in journalism, they are not experts on the topics they are covering. These individuals, who seek out the "truth," also have their own bias which will likely influence the information they collect and share with the world as "fact." They often take information out of context or leave important information out completely—making it appear positive when it is really negative (or vice versa)—aiding in the circulation of misinformation. This purposeful lack of full discloser is a direct reflection of an EQ deficit.

    For example, if a political correspondent states, "We have provided our citizens with over $250 billion in stimulus aid, the most of any country," this is presented as a positive. Viewers will likely use this as ammunition to combat any naysayers who feel we're not offering as much support as other countries.

    However, the whole truth is that, while we may be providing over $250 billion in aid, we are sorely below other countries per capita. What does this mean? If we have 350-million citizens, we are providing each citizen with $714.29 in aid. Whereas, a country providing $120 billion in aid, with a population of 80-million citizens, provides each citizen with $1500 in aid.

    Understandably, we don't have the time to personally fact check everything and discover the contextual nuances. However, there are sources that do this for us. Here are a few (primarily US):

Mediabiasfactcheck.com	Sunlightfoundation.com
Allsides.com	Quoteinvestigator.com
Snopes.com	Factcheck.org

2. **Look for Instant Signs of Bias in False Absolutes**
   As we discussed before, many of us voice our opinion as fact. However, the media—who we rely on to provide us with accurate information—frequently imparts false absolutes. Be on the alert for any absolute statements and what they tell you about the beliefs and opinions of the news outlet.

3. **Name Calling: A Dead Giveaway and a Sign You Should Seek Other Sources of Information**
   When we feel the need to talk negatively about someone and personally attack them, we are displaying a deficit in EQ. Regardless of whether we like a person, a place or thing, name calling, belittling, bullying, and labeling has no place in providing information. For example, stating, "Joe is an idiot and his actions show he is an enemy of the people," is an opinion laced with insult and conspiracy theory. It does not provide useful information for the viewer to make their own judgment. However, reporting that Joe stated XYZ in an interview —verbatim and in full context—, allows people to come to their own conclusion.
   The grand scale at which name calling and labeling is used across the globe, simply shows how many of us lack emotional intelligence and compassion for one another. It does not help that many public officials and influencers—who are seen as individuals to revere and emulate—are propagating this behavior.

4. Don't Let Your Emotions Drive You

When we feel passionately about something, it is easy to get carried away with our emotions. Fear is the emotion that often blinds us the most because it carries with it a host of other unpleasant emotions and feelings like anger, sadness, worry, anxiety, concern, and helplessness. To avoid these feelings, we often dismiss facts and look for a more pleasant and comforting narrative. Climate change is a perfect example of how we may dismiss hard data to avoid addressing our fears and unpleasant emotions that come with observing the potential consequences—which we will talk more about in the upcoming paragraphs.

When we make decisions purely based on our emotions, and someone asks us how we went about concluding what we did, we often have to reverse the process from our feelings. We find things that correspond with the cost-benefit analysis of the conclusion and reconstruct based on the intensity of those feelings we initially had. This is a form of what is called "motivated reasoning." This phenomenon, studied in cognitive science and social psychology, observes us using emotionally-biased reasoning to make decisions (or produce justifications) that are most desired rather than most logical, while still reducing cognitive dissonance (the state of having inconsistent thoughts, beliefs, or attitudes, especially as relating to behavioral decisions and attitude change.)

Consider the controversial topic of climate change. Temperatures are rising everywhere, along with sea levels. And while global warming is cyclical, data shows humans have exacerbated the situation. The fact that some deny global warming all together—natural or otherwise—illustrates how we can choose to turn a blind eye to even scientifically quantified phenomena, often to save ourselves from coming to terms with unexpected consequences, negative feelings, and cognitive dissonance. Another example of this phenomena can be seen in our personal lives. Do you know of someone who has been in, or is in, a toxic or violent relationship? You can't understand why they choose to deny the facts. Yet, this person will justify and dismiss the abuse as "an accident," or their own fault, or even go as far as to defend the person. I use this example because, as much as we want to argue it's only politics, it's not. This issue of seeing what we want to see, and denying what is, is in every facet of our life. And, ultimately, it is our choice whether we feed this unhealthy urge to be right and comfortable—contributing to the EQ deficit.

PREVENTING GROUPTHINK

To be a person purely in search of the truth, even if that means finding out we are wrong, takes courage, confidence, next-level cognition, and humility. We must push past maladaptive traits that encourage us to seek the "answer" (or perceived truth) through our in-group, our resistant ego, and unverified information. Again, this takes effort and energy until we reach a level of unconscious competence.

Unconscious competence (which we discuss in depth in Chapter 15) occurs when we reach a level of mastery such that the skill or behavior becomes second nature, unconscious. At this level of comprehension, it no longer takes effort or drains our energy. An example of unconscious competence may be your ability to speak a foreign language fluently, or the ease with which you can balance on your bike once you have learned how to ride it. However, achieving this level of mastery takes time and effort, which makes getting to this level of competence difficult. Thus, relying on our feelings and our subconscious cognitive shortcuts can be an easy—and potentially disastrous—default.

A healthy first step in seeking out the truth is questioning our thoughts, feelings, and beliefs. In the search for truth, whom or what should we seek out?

The beauty of the world today is that we have all the necessary resources at our disposal. However, the ease of availability of so much information is also a dilemma. To avoid information overload and scouring mountains of data, we tend to rely heavily on our in-group to decide for us, accepting their "truth." For example, some people regard Fox as the only reliable news source and dismiss CNN. Others do exactly the opposite, turning to CNN for a news source that reflects their own belief systems. The truth is, both sources tend to support biased views.

Preventing *groupthink*, which is the practice of thinking or making decisions as a group in a way that discourages creativity or individual responsibility[34], is important in ensuring we do not fall prey to the dangers of tribalism.

It's important for us to acknowledge that, although we have endless amounts of data at our fingertips, it does not make us experts. As Tom Nichols states so eloquently in his book, *The Death of Expertise*:

"...the Internet has accelerated the collapse of communication between experts and laypeople by offering an apparent shortcut to erudition. It allows people to mimic intellectual accomplishment by indulging in an illusion of expertise provided by a limitless supply of facts.

Facts, as experts know, are not the same as knowledge or ability. And, on the Internet, 'facts' are sometimes not even facts.

...the Internet is like artillery support: a constant bombardment of random, disconnected information that rains down on experts and ordinary citizens alike, deafening all of us while blowing up attempts at reasonable discussion."[35]

How to Avoid Groupthink:

1. **Identify the source of your belief**
   For example: Do you carry the same beliefs that were instilled in you at a young age?

2. **Have you ever explored alternative beliefs or tried to debunk bias?**
   Some people are afraid to learn more about other's beliefs because they feel they are being disloyal to their in-group. Learning about other beliefs and ways of doing things does not make you a traitor, and it does not mean you can't stick with your existing beliefs. However, if we do not educate ourselves on alternative perspectives, we cannot claim that we are open-minded or well informed.

   When debunking bias, be careful you do not look for things that prove your existing belief. Instead, look for things that disprove your belief. This will deter us from confirmation bias.

3. **Befriend others who think differently than you do**
   Who says you can't be friends with someone that has different opinions and perspectives than you do? Getting to know someone at a personal level changes the negative stereotypes we often hold about others. It can be an eye-opening experience.

4. **Notice any resistance**
   When it comes to changing our perspective and beliefs our ego has a difficult time relinquishing control. Notice when you are

resistant to understanding alternative views and ask yourself: *Why am I resistant?* Employ emotional intelligence in your processing of this resistance and awareness of the feelings that arise when you think of alternative perspectives.

MORE EMOTIONAL THAN RATIONAL

Although we have evolved to be rational thinkers, our emotional brain still tends to override our analytical skills. For example, people often buy based on emotion and then rationalize their decision. It is usually only after we make our initial decision, based on how it makes us feel, that we then rationalize why we did so. This type of reasoning reaches far beyond how we make purchases.

While reading this section, you may have thought to yourself, "I'm smart enough to not allow these irrational ways of thinking to influence my decisions." You wouldn't be alone in that belief. Specifically, 95% of people who were surveyed believed they were self-aware. They believed they could accurately assess their emotions, understand the source of their feelings, and accurately assess how other people viewed them. However, only 15% of individuals were accurate in their assessment of themselves.[36]

BEING SMART DOESN'T MAKE US RATIONAL

I know a lot of smart people who make very irrational decisions and I know not so intelligent people who make very thoughtful decisions. While on social media, it always shocks me how many people stand by things that are clearly hypocritical to their professed core beliefs and values. I think, "How on earth have they convinced themselves this is even remotely ethical, moral, and bettering humanity?" Yet, they will always find a way to back their position, or instead they'll become highly defensive. Unfortunately, this seems to be a norm in society today.

This is just one reason why developing our emotional intelligence is crucial. Being able to override our primal impulses and irrational ways of thinking is key to reversing a dysfunctional, uncooperative society.

Techniques to Override Our Primal Impulse to Defend and Protect our Ego

There are various techniques out there to lessen the chance of getting into a fiery argument and to take control of our emotions. And while they may work—in theory—they are unlikely to be the first thing that comes to mind in the moment. This is because these techniques often require a clear, rational mind, and, when we become defensive or upset, we are no longer thinking rationally. Like a switch, we flip like Dr. Jekyll to Mr. Hyde, because we have entered an instinctual state to self-protect. In the modern world, that state seems to be to defend our beliefs. Emotional intelligence allows us to be aware of when this switch occurs. Knowing we are less likely to think rationally, we can take the following steps to transition back into a rational state of mind and have a sensible conversation.

1. **Acknowledge you are in an emotionally aroused state.**
   Here are a few signs to tell when we have transitioned into this state:
   - The feeling of unpleasant emotions. You may feel anger, resentment, appalled, intimidated, panicky, humiliated, ridiculed, rejected, judged, trapped, etc.
   - Increased heart rate
   - Shallow breathing

- The urge to defend
- Spontaneous perspiration

2. **Acknowledge this is not the time to react, although this is exactly what you want to do.**

3. **Don't listen if you can't. Make the choice to either listen or acknowledge you are in no state to have the conversation now.** This does not mean we should completely avoid the conversation. However, we first must transition into a neutral state of mind, otherwise we will not be able to effectively listen and come from a place of understanding. If we choose to listen:
   - Take a deep breath.
   - Seek to learn something.
   - Be aware if you find yourself seeking out how they are "wrong"—this hinders understanding.
   - Look for the message behind their emotion—we will dive deeper into this in Chapter 14: The Hidden Message.
   - Do not interrupt.
   - Ask questions to gain a deeper understanding, but avoid questions laced with judgment.
   - Provide a summary of what you heard them say and ask for clarification.

   If you realize you are in no state to have the conversation:
   - Voice this to the other person(s) involved. For example, you might say, "[person's name] when discussing [X] I notice I am becoming [feeling or emotion] and when I am in this state I'm unable to hear what you are saying. I need a moment to [calm down/breathe/get into the right state of mind] before I can have this discussion with you."

If met with hostility—after voicing your need to take a moment—decide if this is an appropriate conversation to have with this person. If there is no mutual respect, chances are, it will not be a productive conversation.

- Find compassion for the other person or find appreciation for something else in your life. This will allow you to lower your heart rate and find something positive to focus on.

4. Fully take responsibility for how you respond.

5. Acknowledge your emotions but do not let them lead the conversation with the other person.

EMOTIONS ALONE MAKE US VULNERABLE

When we feel threatened, unheard, or misunderstood, emotions run high and we tend to cling more strongly to our currently held beliefs, looking for a safe haven with the people and information that supports us (our tribe). Anything or anyone outside of that "safe zone" we perceive as a threat.

Because we are biological organisms, it is our nature to defend against foreign objects, which we can generalize to defending ourselves against foreign beliefs. Sadly, some people seek to benefit from our biological nature, and we often become pawns in their game. Today's politicians and influencers are two simple examples.

How do you determine if a message is manipulative, dogmatic, and biased? Look for the following telltale signs:

1. The speaker positions the opposing person or group as the villain.

2. The speaker labels veritable information as propaganda.

3. The speaker dismisses his or her shortcomings and often blames them on others, typically the opposing individual or group.

4. The speaker tends to focus more on blame than on solving a common problem.

5. The speaker is quick to assign negative labels to others (idiot, evil, enemy) or generalize (all people who associate with X group or individual are to blame).

The lack of our social-emotional literacy is allowing us to fall prey to the corrupt systems around us. The systems we feel should have our best interests at heart. The systems which are ultimately using our archaic behavioral tendencies to influence us to work against one another. Therefore, I stress the importance of understanding emotions. We deserve to understand why we make the choices we make; feel the way we feel, and not fall victim to deception or self-destruction. Being in tune with our emotions is far from a weakness. On the contrary, being able to understand our emotions, control them, and communicate our needs and that of others is a powerful skill.

8

The Mechanics of the Mind

"The mind is a powerful force. It can enslave us or empower us. It can plunge us into the depths of misery or take us to the heights of ecstasy. Learn to use the power wisely."

— **David Cuschieri**

Mind: the element of a person that enables them to be aware of the world and their experiences, to think, and to feel; the faculty of consciousness and thought.[37]

Based on our perceptions and mindset, our moods and behaviors can fluctuate quickly. Henry Ford once said, "Whether you think you can, or you think you can't, you're right."

Our thoughts are powerful. Not only do they alter how we perceive the world around us and influence our emotions, they also alter our biology. In this chapter, we will take a deep dive into the power of the mind and how to control it to ensure optimal well-being and a healthy view of the people and things around us.

MANIFESTATION OF THOUGHT

Take a moment to close your eyes and think a thought that makes you feel a strong and powerful emotion (this could be positive or negative). For one to two minutes, immerse yourself in thought and the feelings and emotions that arise.

What was the thought? What specifically did you feel? Was the feeling so strong it made you feel as though you were experiencing the situation? Did your heartbeat feel different? Did your breathing change? What was the feeling in your gut?

It's remarkable that we can escape our reality by simply thinking about something. While we can use such thoughts to make us feel happier, thinking can be quite dreadful for those who use their thoughts to create their own hell on Earth.

WHAT HAPPENS WHEN WE THINK A THOUGHT?

The results of a thought depend on the thought itself. If we think about a gory movie, we can literally feel sick to our stomach. Thinking of a favorite pastime may trigger a feeling of warmth and activate the memory of senses such as a smell or taste. Even imaginary thought or thought of a future event can alter our state of being. For example, when you think of a hypothetical situation, it will evoke the same emotions and feelings as if you were to experience it in real time. Our thoughts manifest both physically and emotionally. In fact, there is a field of study solely dedicated to studying the mind-body connection: *psychoneuroimmunology*. What exactly happens to us physically when we think a thought?

Generating a thought creates a biochemical reaction in our brain, starting with a wave of electrical impulses that pass through our brain circuits. The impulses, unique to that thought, generate a chemical reaction that releases chemical messages, called *neurotransmitters*, throughout our body that match our thoughts. If we have a pleasant thought, those neurotransmitters are likely to consist of dopamine, serotonin, oxytocin, and endorphins ("happy" hormones) that match our thoughts to our emotions and our bodies.

The result is a feedback loop of thought, feel, emotion, thought (repeat).

Although this process may seem very straightforward and systematic, it is extremely complicated. In processing our thoughts, our brain engages various "departments" or brain structures, such as the prefrontal cortex (rational brain, reasoning), hippocampus (center for memory), and amygdala (emotions and behavior), simultaneously. Most of these processes run in the background (our subconscious), which accounts for approximately 90% of our cognitive functioning.

Let's look at a specific example. Assume your spouse is late getting home from work. You begin to think of reasons why they might be running late—traffic, for example. But, as time passes, and your phone calls and texts go unanswered, you start to worry. Subconsciously, your brain is analyzing data, sorting through various scenarios, possibilities, past experiences, and emotions associated with similar situations that assist you in forming various hypotheses. While this is happening, you become aware of how you feel, which leads to further thought.

Depending on your relationship with your spouse, the reasons you imagine for their tardiness may vary. If your spouse is rarely late and always calls to let you know, you may be more inclined to worry. That feeling of worry triggers thoughts of concern, which then releases neurotransmitters related to anxiety, such as norepinephrine, glutamate, and gamma-amino butyric acid (GABA), that physically manifest within your body. Your breathing may become shallow, your heart rate may speed up, and you might feel sick to your stomach, which causes you to worry more. Now you may begin to think, "Were they involved in an accident?" Then you think about what an accident might entail, and you end up sending yourself into a feedback loop of worry.

However, if you are suspicious of your spouse and things haven't been going well in the relationship, these past experiences and thoughts can generate a completely different reaction in the body. You may still feel sick to your stomach, anxious, and short of breath, but might feel anger instead of worry.

Once your spouse is home, the feelings and emotions that were triggered by your thoughts will greatly determine how you react when they walk in the door. If you were worried, you may greet them with a big bear hug and a kiss, explaining how concerned you were. However, if you had thoughts that your spouse may have been late due to infidelity, you might react with accusations, anger, and inter-rogation.

But, what if the simple truth was that they were pulled into a last-minute meeting at work and were unable to step away to call you? And what if they forgot to charge their phone, so they didn't receive any of your messages? In this case, neither of your possible re-sponses were based on the actual truth of the matter.

"Reality is built out of thought, and our every thought begins to create reality."
— Edgar Cayce

GETTING INSIDE OUR HEADS

To better understand how we think, feel, and operate, it's important to have a basic understanding of the functions and anatomy of our brains.

The human brain evolved from the bottom up. The brainstem, which is connected to the spinal cord, controls the basic bodily func-tions that keep us alive; and the cerebellum is responsible for movement and coordination. The brainstem and the cerebellum are the oldest and most basic aspects of the brain, which we humans share with reptiles; hence why it is often referred to as the "reptilian brain."

As we continued to evolve, we developed the emotional and behavioral components of the brain known as the limbic system, which is unique to mammals. When we recall warm, fuzzy feelings about a loved one or furry creature, or when we feel envy when our neighbor wins the lottery, the limbic system is at work. There are two primary components of the limbic system: the amygdala and the hippocampus.

Both the amygdala and the hippocampus are responsible for encoding (interpreting input from our senses), storing, and recalling memories, but they are responsible for slightly different aspects of those memories.

When evoking a memory, you may recall what the environment was like—the smells, tastes, and sounds—and you may also recall feelings that were associated with that experience or memory. Let's use a trip to a tropical island as an example. The hippocampus, which I like to refer to as the "objective encoder", manages the perceived "facts" of the event. Was it hot, warm, humid? Can you recall the sunshine on your face and the sand between your toes? What about the refreshing taste of a tropical smoothie?

These senses and memories are housed in the hippocampus. Tied to those sensory memories, you may recall a feeling of contentment and happiness; these aspects of the event are stored in the amygdala, or the "subjective encoder." Together, the hippocampus and the amygdala create the full experience, both the context and emotions associated with the memory. They also assist us in deciding how to respond to future events based on the context and emotions of past experiences. For example, when we see a bear, our amygdala may want to react with fear. However, simultaneously, the hippocampus is analyzing the context of where we see that bear, ensuring we respond appropriately. If the bear is at the zoo, it would be inappropriate for us to react with fear; if it's a grizzly bear in the wild, however, it would be highly appropriate to react with fear.

And, finally, we have the neocortex, sometimes called the "rational brain." Your neocortex allows you to read and comprehend the words on a page. It allows us to contemplate, rationalize, and problem-solve. As far as we know, it has unlimited learning capabilities. Without this center of the brain, societies, culture, and technologies could not exist.

These various components (brainstem, limbic system, and neocortex) work together, not in isolation of one another, but simultaneously. They are constantly checking in with one another to ensure the correct feelings are felt and the correct actions are being taken. Our experiences, feelings, thoughts, and responses all work together to create the full experience.

Yet, there are those moments when our "rational brain" doesn't get invited to the party and our emotions move from being a copilot to taking over the controls.

A WORLD OF IMAGINATION

As the previous example shows, we often react to situations before we know the whole story. Rather, we react based on the "reality" we create in our minds. And, once we have created our own form of reality, it is hard to talk ourselves back down to the reality that is in front of us—even if it is a more informed perspective.

The human imagination is powerful. You may be able to think back to your childhood when something as simple as a stick could be transformed into almost anything; a sword, a microphone, a light saber, or a magic wand. A slide in the park may have been a magical portal to a different world.

Although our imagination may seem to wane as we transition into adulthood, it is still very much alive and arguably more powerful. As children, we used it primarily for play, but as adults we use our imagination (subconsciously) to alter our known reality. Understanding how our minds operate allows us to navigate between the narratives we create in our own minds and the objective reality of the situation.

ALTERED MEMORIES

Why is it that two people who experienced the exact same event recall it very differently?

Mark and Allison are an entrepreneurial couple in their mid-30's who met in grad school, according to Allison, and at a local bar, according to Mark. As I sat across from them in a quaint coffee bar in South End, Charlotte, the two couldn't be more in sync when it comes to the direction they want to take their business. However, I was fascinated to hear their drastically different and detailed accounts of how they first met. Both were convinced of the accuracy of their memories and both were shocked that the other was so far off the mark.

The variation in memory between witnesses tends to increase when the parties involved have vastly different attitudes toward the given situation. For example, if you have ever listened to a couple recount the chain of events leading up to an argument and how it unfolded, you are likely to hear very different stories as to who started the argument, who raised their voice first, what the argument was initially about, and so on. The more people disagree, the more you can bet their stories will not align.

Sometimes we knowingly alter the facts to win the argument or to avoid cognitive dissonance. However, when we recall a situation and are recounting the story, we usually believe that it happened as we say it happened. We may even have visual and auditory memories to support our case. Unfortunately, no one can see inside of our heads, and it is difficult to know for certain that our memories are accurate.

The Process of Forming Memories

Memories are associated with feelings, and feelings influence our perception. Let's explore how this occurs. Our perception and feelings interpret our sensory input, which is then encoded as a memory and stored in two areas of the brain: the hippocampus (memory and learning center) and amygdala (feelings and emotions center). Simultaneously, we experience top-down processing. Top-down processing pulls from our prior experiences and knowledge of similar situations to help us determine how to perceive and feel about current or future events. Cognitive bias and beliefs also play a major role in our perception. Put simply, our perception is our reality alone and is stored as such in our memory, which explains why we can recall something completely different from other bystanders.

Filters

Our world is filled with data, with our body sending approximately 11-million bits per second to the brain. Yet our brains can only process an estimated 50-80 bits per second.[38] That is an infinitesimal amount considering all there is to experience in the sensory world. What does this limitation mean for our memory? It means we must filter. We subconsciously pick and choose what information we want to keep, and we throw the rest out the window, so to speak.

For example, many of us have felt self-conscious about how others perceive us. When we are feeling insecure, and assume we are being judged by everyone around us, an innocent glance from another person can make us feel that they are critiquing how we look. A laughing couple at the table behind us may make us feel we are being mocked, literally behind our backs.

We frequently seek to prove ourselves right. Often, whatever we are looking for to confirm our beliefs, we are sure to find. If we believe today will be an amazing day, it likely will be, because we will find things to be grateful for. The smallest of things that reinforce the idea that today is a great day becomes our proof: the smell of food, ample sunshine, birds chirping, enjoying music or a good book, or chatting with a friend or loved one. Similarly, if we assume it is going to be a terrible day, we are likely to focus on the frustrations we experience throughout our day (no matter how small) to prove that our expectations were accurate. In other words, we have created a self-fulfilling prophecy.

Let's try a simple experiment. Find and focus on things around you that are yellow. Give yourself a minute or two to identify everything you can see that is yellow. Now, without cheating, close your eyes and recall everything around you that is blue.

Did you find it difficult to recall the things around you that are blue because you had set your focus on the things that are yellow?

The point being, we control how we choose to view and interact with the world around us and inside of us. People can do and say things to us, things can happen all around us, but we (and only we) control what we choose to focus on and how we feel about every circumstance and situation.

To develop our emotional intelligence, we must become aware of and accept the fact that we are in full control of our thoughts and emotions. But what happens when we base our feelings and emotions solely on our recollection of the event? Are our memories sound enough to use them as supporting evidence when making a judgment on how we should feel?

Manipulated and Fabricated Memories

It seems almost worthy of science fiction that someone could manipulate us into creating artificial memories, but it happens, and it is, eerily, easy to do. In the 1990s, cases began to surface of implanted memories. Many of the cases were situations where psychotherapists were treating patients with depression or extreme trust issues. Through guided questioning (which is not an accepted practice in psychology), the therapist began to imply that their client may have suffered trauma as a child, and that the trauma led to their fears, trust issues, and severe depression. By asking patients to recall such traumatic events, they began to develop artificial memories. And, in some cases, innocent people were sent to prison for crimes they did not commit based on these.

Dr. Elizabeth Loftus, a cognitive psychologist and expert on human memory, conducted hundreds of experiments to test how existing memories can be manipulated and how fictitious memories can be implanted. Her conclusion? Twenty-five percent of the participants in her study were convinced they had experienced a traumatic event that never in fact occurred.[39] For example, a young woman vividly recalled jumping off her family's two-story roof with an umbrella, as a child, and floating gracefully down like Mary Poppins. This, of course, is physically impossible. The fall would be anything but graceful and would likely result in broken limbs and other life-threatening injuries.

Another disproven memory comes from a man who recalls—at age twelve—watching the terrorist attacks of 9/11 from his mother's apartment window across the Hudson River in New Jersey. He recalls, in detail, watching as the smoke made its way across the city and the river. Yet, this wasn't possible because his mother didn't move to New York until four years after 9/11.

Dreams, news, pictures, and stories told by others, can all contribute to the development of false memories. Our brains can easily take in this sensory information, as if we ourselves are experiencing it. Thus, we may squirm or cringe at the sight of a nasty wound or surgical procedure on a TV show, get anxious for the characters who are running for their lives in a thriller, or shed tears while reading about a character who is suffering a great loss or tragedy.

MEMORY: IN CONCLUSION

If memories are based on our perception of the world around us, and we can only process mere fractions of the sensory input we experience, and that input can later be altered … can we really trust ourselves?

By developing our emotional intelligence, we can go into a situation with a heightened sense of awareness, becoming more observant of our sensory environment and the emotions, feelings, and past experiences that may alter our perception. Even if we do slip up and make an inaccurate observation (as we inevitably will), we are less likely to become defensive and more likely to be open to alternative points of view.

WE ARE WHAT WE THINK

You may be familiar with the saying: "You are what you eat." The same is true of our thoughts. The way we think influences our bodies' chemistry, affecting our physical health and overall well-being. Our thoughts quite literally feed our body with a cocktail of chemicals composed of neurotransmitters, peptides (act as structural components of cells and tissues, hormones, toxins, antibiotics, and enzymes), and hormones that impact how our bodies feel and function. Healthy emotions are like a healthy diet. We know these chemicals correlate with our feelings and can affect our autonomic nervous system (our heart rate, respiratory rate, digestion— the system that controls all the things we don't have to consciously think about doing), and alter trillions of cells within our body. But just how impactful are these emotional cocktails?

HAPPY AND HEALTHY

Studies have shown that individuals who are able to control their thoughts and regulate their emotions are more resilient during times of chaos, stress, and uncertainty. As the saying goes, we may not be able to control the situation, but we can control how we respond to the situation.

In addition to helping us bounce back from a tough situation, thinking positive and caring thoughts has been shown to improve our immune system; reduce our risk of heart disease by 30%; improve clarity, memory and problem-solving ability; promote healthier relationships; and increase DHEA (a hormone that can help with depression, anti-aging, obesity, adrenal insufficiency and also counters the effects of cortisol). [40] Given these benefits, why do some people seem to seek out and thrive on doom, gloom, and unpleasant moods? It could be that these circumstances produce adrenaline and can resemble excitement. Or it could be we are "comfortable" living in a state we are all too familiar with.

HOMEOSTASIS OF MOOD

Homeostasis is the tendency toward a relatively stable balance between interdependent elements, especially physiological processes. In terms of how we feel, we all seem to have a baseline response toward situations that is part of our inborn demeanor. We can think of this natural state of being as our default mood. While our mood can fluctuate up or down based on stimulants and situations, we always seem to find our way back to our baseline. The question is: Can we change our default mood?

Many scientists say yes. Mood is dictated largely by the body's natural chemicals, and because our thoughts directly affect what chemicals are released in the brain, then it makes sense that if we change our state of being, we can change our default mood.

The key is to be patient with ourselves and realize that it takes time to change deep-rooted behaviors and habits. We naturally favor environments we are familiar with, even if they are toxic—because we know what to expect. We become addicted to feeling a certain way, and changes to that state of being may make us feel worse rather than better.

Suppose you are a coffee drinker, and you've been guzzling five hefty cups of non-decaf coffee every day for the past 15 years or so. Your body is now accustomed to high amounts of caffeine daily. If, one day, you decide to switch to decaf coffee, your body will likely feel the impacts immediately. In contrast, if you gradually cut back on your caffeine consumption over time, your body will eventually adjust to a new normal without experiencing caffeine withdrawals.

The same is true for emotions. We must wean ourselves off the negative stimuli around us. For example, if you wake up and digest the latest news, first thing in the morning, instead try avoiding the media and replacing with a positive or educational podcast. If you notice you spend your weekends around friends who are prone to gossip, you could look to spend time in a healthier emotional environment.

When you do make these adjustments, notice the shift in your mood and behavior throughout the day. What changed? Do you react to situations differently?

TOXIC EMOTIONS

Stress is unavoidable and essential to our survival. A burst of adrenaline when we become startled triggers a fight-or-flight response, intended to promote survival. Unfortunately, our survival mode today is being triggered by situations that are not life threatening. These situations might include stressful work environments, demanding deadlines, unhealthy relationships, and the pressure to conform to social norms. Chemicals that were intended to be short-lived are flooding our bodies. Cortisol, norepinephrine, and epinephrine (also known as adrenaline) affect the constriction of our heart and blood vessels. Experiencing these states of stress for extended and frequent periods of time leaves us stewing in a brew of biological "poison."

This bath of chemicals, brought on by chronic stress, can become toxic, slowly killing us by weakening our immune system and opening the door to illness and disease. Our chances of heart disease are significantly increased by high cortisol levels that raise our blood pressure, cholesterol, triglycerides, and blood sugar; we may suffer from fatigue, trouble sleeping, difficulties focusing, poor memory, weight gain or loss, change in appetite, lower energy levels, and intolerance for others. While experiencing chronic stress and anxiety, and living in a constant state of survival mode, our cognitive functions can be significantly impaired. In this state, we're much more likely to see things and other people as threats, leading to yet another unhealthy feedback loop.

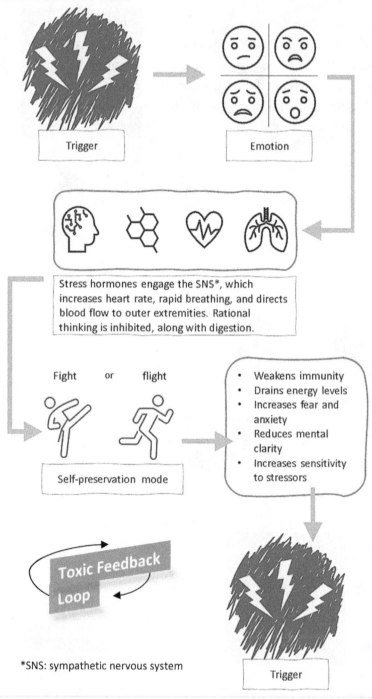

Trigger

Emotion

Stress hormones engage the SNS*, which increases heart rate, rapid breathing, and directs blood flow to outer extremities. Rational thinking is inhibited, along with digestion.

Fight   or   flight

Self-preservation mode

- Weakens immunity
- Drains energy levels
- Increases fear and anxiety
- Reduces mental clarity
- Increases sensitivity to stressors

Toxic Feedback Loop

*SNS: sympathetic nervous system

Trigger

Being in a constant state of toxic emotion is exhausting. Our bodies were never meant to endure these feelings and execute survival responses for long periods of time. When the sympathetic nervous system (rapid heart rate, survival mode) has been exhausted, we rely more heavily on the parasympathetic nervous system (rest and digest). At that point, feelings of burnout, being overwhelmed, and depression may start presenting themselves.

Individuals often resort to prescription medication to ease their suffering. Antianxiety medications and antidepressants mimic the "feel-good" neurotransmitters, and they can help lift us out of our slump or calm us down in times of panic. Unfortunately, these medications cannot take care of the underlying causes of our depression or anxiety. Though we feel better, something is still missing, which suggests that medications should be a short-term solution while we focus on addressing the root causes of these symptoms.

Speaking from personal experience, I always thought I was just a naturally anxious and stressed-out person. I was told that "it runs in the family" and that I had a chemical imbalance. Both statements were true, but not for the reasons you might think. Yes, anxiety and depression do run in my family, but those who experienced them also lack the emotional intelligence to overcome and to properly address their emotions. I did have a chemical imbalance, but it was because I was creating my imbalance.

We often feel helpless and trapped. But we unknowingly set most of these traps and limitations ourselves. Becoming aware of this vicious cycle and learning how to regulate our emotions (which we will discuss in upcoming chapters) is at the root of developing emotional intelligence. We begin to understand that we aren't bad people, and that we aren't broken or trapped either; we are simply reacting to environmental and psychological stimulants. When we do gain control of our thoughts, we can take back control of our mind and body.

The process of re-correcting years of negative feedback loops and habitual unproductive behavior takes time. We need to have patience with ourselves and others during the process, which can be difficult, especially in a day and age when life seems more demanding of our time and energy, and attention spans are ever waning.

RAPID CUTS: HOW TECHNOLOGY REWIRES OUR BRAINS

Time in front of a TV screen was limited when I stayed with my grandparents. They would always tell me, "If you keep staring at that screen, you brain is going to rot." I remember on several occasions my grandmother walking over, turning off the television, and telling me not to "waste a beautiful day by being cooped up inside, staring at a screen," or to "find something more stimulating to do, like a puzzle or reading a book".

Screen time has always been a concern, mainly because it takes children (and now adults) away from interacting with the world and people around them, leading to lower levels of engagement and problem-solving. Today, television, video games, and other rapid-frame stimulants have changed the way we process and attend to the world and activities around us.

When you sit down to watch your favorite show, or happen to see a commercial, I encourage you to take note of how many times the screen cuts from one frame to another. How do these rapid cuts affect us? The more time we spend in front of a screen, digesting rapid stimulation, the more likely we are to suffer from attention disorders.

We often wonder why children (and now many adults) have such a difficult time concentrating and staying focused. Numerous studies have been conducted to determine the links between screen time, attention-deficit disorder (ADD) and attention-deficit/hyperactivity disorder (ADHD). Although we do not know whether excessive screen time can *cause* ADD/ADHD, there is a significant correlation between the amount of screen time consumed by participants in this research, and symptoms related to ADD/ADHD, including behavioral issues and shorter attention spans.

For example, a study conducted at the University of Alberta found that children who spend more than two hours (per day) in front of a screen by the age of five, were 7.7 times more likely to meet the criteria for a diagnosis of attention deficit hyperactivity disorder compared to children who spent 30 minutes or less each day in front of a screen.[41]

Even if our screen time was limited when we were children, it is likely that, as adults, we have had enough exposure to "rapid" technology that our brains are just as prone to have reduced attention spans.

THE "NEED" TO BE CONSTANTLY ENTERTAINED

Do you ever feel bombarded by constant stimulation? Who would have ever imagined that, when pumping gas, you would be able to watch television from the gas pump, or through the vanity mirror in public restrooms? Warren Buffett once said, "I insist on a lot of time being spent, almost every day, to just sit and think. That is very uncommon in American business." Not only is uninterrupted time uncommon in American business, it is equally uncommon in everyday life, where it can be difficult to escape the bombardment of constant stimulation.

As much as we like to glamorize multitasking, we can only give our full attention to one thing at a time. Multitasking is really a juggling act, switching from one task or thought to the other in rapid succession. However, studies have shown that multitasking is much less effective than bringing one task to completion before starting a new task.

Here's an activity to help you understand how multitasking works— or doesn't. You will need a piece of paper, something to write with, and a stopwatch. For the first part of the activity, write down your first name and last name. Use the stopwatch to identify the amount of time that elapsed between the writing of the first letter of your first name and the last letter of your last name. Record the time.

In the second half of the activity, you are also going to write your full name, but you are going to alternate between the letters of your first name and last name. For example, if your name is Jane Doe, you would start with writing the letter J followed by the first letter of your last name D, alternating back and forth until both first and last name are completed. You will likely find that it takes nearly twice as long to complete this activity.

To explain, the writing of each name in this activity represents a task. Completing one task at a time (i.e. writing your first name followed by your last name) is more efficient than alternating back and forth from one task to another (as in the second part of the activity) which represents multitasking.

Thus, while it may seem we can do two things at once, we can't. Our brain is simply hopping from one area of focus to another. We cannot be fully attentive to our surroundings when we are immersed in our devices, or fully present and in the moment when our attention is being stolen by stimulants like television at gas pumps. We are less likely to be in a state of thought and introspection. These seemingly minuscule amounts of time could be put to better use.

One of the best ways to avoid our attention being robbed by these distractions is to eliminate them. If you know you are likely to pick up your phone when you need to focus on or enjoy something else, leave your device far enough out of reach that it becomes an inconvenience to grab it. Try going for a walk with your device turned off and take in your surroundings. Practice mindfulness, becoming aware of your thoughts, feelings, and senses. All these things will aid in developing your emotional intelligence through self-awareness.

While we have become accustomed to "living" through a screen, and are eager to capture the special moments in our lives, our reliance on our devices to do the documenting is affecting our personal encoding of the moment and the emotions we once associated with these special experiences.

DO YOU REMEMBER...?

Reflection and time spent in the present moment are in scarce supply these days. There is the illusion that we have no time for reflection, when the truth is, we are not *making* time.

Technology seems to be replacing the need for rote processing (memorization). If you were born before 1990, you probably recall, to this day, your home phone number, along with the phone numbers of a handful of friends and relatives. Yet today, with the ability to program names and numbers into our devices, there is no need to remember such information. Unfortunately, if we lose our phones, the odds of being able to get in touch with an important person in our life are low.

Similarly, GPS systems have replaced the need to create a mental map of our surroundings and a sense of direction. Calculators have long since replaced our need to understand mathematical calculations. And today's social media and "documentary" technologies seem to be replacing our need to mentally store our experiences.

Studies have shown that individuals who rely on technology to capture their experiences are much less likely to recall those memories accurately, or the feelings associated with them. Emma Templeton, a psychological researcher from Dartmouth College, led a study in which 100 participants were led through a self-guided tour of a church and asked to pay close attention to the details of their experience. Some of the participants were permitted to use technology to capture their experience, while others were "unarmed" and solely reliant on their memories. A week later, participants were quizzed on the details of the visit. Templeton reports that, "Participants without media consistently remembered their experience more precisely than participants who used media ... These findings suggest that using media may prevent people from remembering the very events they are attempting to preserve." [42]

Documenting our experiences can also display an exaggerated and unrealistic depiction of our life and others' lives. When we spend so much time trying to get the right angle, expression, and pose, we are not only taking time away from being present and in the moment, we are likely creating artificial moods, appearing happier or more content than we are actually feeling.

As noted earlier, our memories are easily manipulated and altered. When we skim through our documented experiences (which are often exaggerated depictions of an experience), we may believe we were happier in that moment than we were. We also wonder why we don't feel as happy now as we once did. This can cause depression, envy of others, FOMO (fear of missing out), and a feeling of emptiness. The reality is, we were likely not happier then than we are now. Instead, we depicted a fraudulent happiness in our photo shoot, which I like to call "counterfeit candids".

The modern obsession with *capturing* the moment is paradoxically causing us to completely miss the beauty that comes from truly *living* in the moment. We are depriving ourselves of the experiences and feelings that we long for by trying so desperately to document them. Next time you have the urge to do this, notice the time you spend trying to capture the "perfect" photo, compared to the time you spend being present and enjoying the experience.

Ultimately, we are robbing ourselves of the clarity, peace and creativity that comes from solitude, self-reflection, and the natural beauty of the world and people around us.

EMOTIONAL HIJACKING

In his book, *Emotional Intelligence,* psychologist Daniel Goleman refers to our primitive impulse to react to threats (anything that triggers our fight or flight response) as "amygdala hijacking." The amygdala (responsible for emotions) is activated and the neocortex (the rational brain) fails to save us. It produces a sort of *Dr. Jekyll and Mr. Hyde* effect—that split second, hair trigger moment when the "you" that you know becomes unrecognizable. When threatened, we become defensive and words often slip from our lips followed by instant regret, lighting-fast reflexes send our fists flying toward someone or something, or we impulsively pull the trigger, all initiated by our primitive urge to react.

Although most moments of outrage do not end in someone dying, the sad truth is that most homicides (by guns) are caused by impulsive reactions to situations. Although our anger or words may not have killed anyone, the emotional hijacking propels the action. Those raised in an environment where emotional impulse trumps rational thinking are much more inclined to react first and think later. This is all the more reason for us to understand how to control, refine, and harness the power of our emotions and mind.

Here are some strategies for controlling our urge to react on impulse:

1. **Know your triggers**

   When we know what triggers us, we can either (1) avoid situations where we will become triggered, or (2) mentally prepare for how to properly handle triggers when they occur.

2. **Mentally rehearse the situation**

   Visualize yourself in a situation where you may be triggered. How do you feel? How will you respond—with emotional intelligence?

   Mental rehearsal is a highly effective method, not only for regulating our emotions, but also improving our performance. Athletes who visualize a play and rehearse different scenarios in their mind—in addition to practice—have been found to be much more agile and effective than those who simply practice on the field.

3. **Verbally acknowledge your faults**

   Often, when we experience emotional hijacking, rational processing goes out the window. We don't think about breathing, stepping away, or the consequences of our actions. However, if we have developed awareness, we can quickly recognize when we have made a mistake or misspoken. Verbally acknowledge it when this happens, and course correct. For example: "I'm sorry for what I just did/said. That was spoken out of [name feeling]. What I meant to say was...."

When we can acknowledge and take control of our emotions, we also control the energy that is associated with our emotions.

9

E-motion: Energy in Motion

"Everything is energy and that is all there is to it. Match the frequency of the reality you want, and you cannot help but get that reality. It can be no other way. This is not philosophy. This is physics."

— **Albert Einstein**

Have you ever felt a surge of panic when you see the "low battery" or "critical battery" alert on your phone or device, especially when there is not a charger nearby? Fortunately, our devices have been designed to go into "low battery mode" when they're running low on power. Most of the time, the power runs down because we forgot to close the applications that we aren't using.

Like our devices, we too have a "battery" that loses energy when it is overstressed. For us to stay charged and prevent our energy source from going into critical mode, we must manage our energy wisely by eliminating things that drain us and finding things that charge us. Those "background apps" in our lives can be small, but they add up. In this chapter, we'll not only discuss how our emotions affect our mood and energy, we will look at ways to better manage our energy, identify and eliminate energy drainers, and find sources to renew our energy levels.

HOW ENERGY LEVELS AFFECT MOOD

If you have ever come home from a stressful day, you may have noticed that your tolerance for mild irritants is much lower than normal. The dog that jumps on you when you arrive, eager to be taken out and fed, the children running and screaming around the house, the dirty dishes in the sink; all of these can easily trigger strong negative emotions, which you may have otherwise overlooked or repressed. Repressing unpleasant emotions takes energy, and when our energy is already at a critically low level, it can be nearly impossible to hold back.

An important part of emotional intelligence is the ability to be aware of our triggers—the situations and occurrences that drain our energy. When we know what sucks the energy out of us and "pushes our buttons" we can control how we let them affect us.

ASSESSING TOLERANCES

Identifying all our triggers and tolerances can be tricky. Many of our energy drainers can go unnoticed, living in our subconscious due to their seeming triviality. We often believe we cannot eliminate many of the things we find stressful but which we tolerate, so we just deal with them, knowing that they're always there in the background, like those open apps on our devices. However, we have more control over them than we may think. It's simply a matter of recognizing them and deciding to address as many as possible. Below are 50 examples of irritations you may be tolerating. Check all that apply to you and add to the list if necessary. As you begin to eliminate these from your life, you may find it helpful to keep a journal on any changes you notice in your mood, energy, and relationships.

Things You May Be Tolerating

- ○ Excessive clutter
- ○ Limited storage space
- ○ Pet hair you can't seem to get rid of
- ○ Notifications on your phone or computer that interrupt you
- ○ A dirty car with limited trunk space
- ○ A room that needs repainting
- ○ An unkept lawn that you find to be an eyesore
- ○ Wearing clothes that aren't comfortable
- ○ Wearing uncomfortable shoes
- ○ A bad hair day
- ○ Cleaning the litter box
- ○ A house in need of repairs
- ○ The sound of someone eating
- ○ A box or bag of donations that needs to be dropped off
- ○ Noticeable dust collecting on surfaces
- ○ Missing your favorite show or game
- ○ Credit card debt
- ○ Doctors' appointments
- ○ Needy family or friends
- ○ Dings or dents in your vehicle

○ Pet poop in your yard

○ Not making enough money to afford what you want or need

○ Living in an area where you don't feel safe

○ Snow that needs shoveling

○ A printer that is jammed or ran out of ink

○ Lack of adequate lighting

○ Uncomfortable thermostat settings

○ Working at a job that you do not enjoy

○ Trash or recycling needing to be taken out

○ A slow or offline network

○ The demands of being a parent

○ Toothache or other physical discomfort

○ Traffic on your daily commute

○ Spending too much time online

○ Student loan debt

○ Having a shattered or cracked screen

○ Unwanted body fat

○ Being hungry but too tired to stop and pick up food

○ Feeling obligated to buy gifts for others

○ A spouse who you feel does not contribute

○ Feeling trapped at your desk for eight hours

○ Difficult, demanding clients

○ A website or app needing updates

○ A disorganized workspace

○ Telemarketers

○ Limited space on public transportation

○ Laundry in need of washing and folding

○ An uncomfortable pillow

○ A device with a short battery life

○ Watching something you're not interested in to appease someone else

○ Children's needs or demands

What else are you tolerating?

_____

_____

_____

_____

_____

_____

_____

_____

_____

_____

_____

_____

When reading through the list, you may have thought, "But I have no choice but to tolerate ____." A good example is cooking for and bathing your young children. Of course, you have your parental duties, and the burden is even heavier if you are a single parent. Nonetheless, you can find creative ways to improve the situation. For example, you might do meal prep one day and bathing on the next day. It's really about finding what works for you. You might even listen to your favorite tunes while you cook and do other household chores to balance your energy levels.

Everything we do and everything we tolerate in life is a choice. EVERYTHING. It's essential to remember this truism because we must not allow ourselves to adopt a victim mentality. For example, you make the choice to feed and bathe your children because you want them to be healthy, not hungry, and you want them to be clean, not dirty. Of course, you also want to be a good parent. If you stopped feeding and bathing them, you would risk their health and safety, and you might be charged with neglect and child endangerment.

When we take the time to reflect on why we do or tolerate certain things, identifying the choices we are making in the process, we can improve our reactions and responses to people and situations.

When Tolerance is Enabling

Drew considers himself a tolerant person, who refuses to allow minor irritants—like a small mess around the apartment, or a short visit from his roommate's obnoxious friend to unnerve him. However, Drew is starting to feel like his roommate Jay is taking advantage of his easiness.

Early on, Drew established house rules which Jay agreed to. For example: clean up after yourself, be respectful of one another's privacy, notify one another when expecting guests, no late-night guests on weekdays, and no eating food that isn't yours.

The first two months, Jay was a well-mannered and respectful roommate; almost too good to be true. And like most things that seem too good to be true, they usually are. The first incident, Drew recalls, was coming home to a pile of Jay's dirty gym laundry on the corner of the common room couch.

He shrugged it off to a busy schedule, and it was removed later that evening. But then, similar and more frequent messes began to appear; dirty dishes left lying around for 3-5 days straight before being washed; damp laundry left in the washer; and more frequent, unannounced visits from Jay's friends.

However, Drew did not want to disrupt the peace between him and his roommate. He believed addressing the issue would cause far more tension and arguing than simply tolerating Jay's messes and friends.

To ease his anxiety and frustration, Drew began to spend more time away from his apartment. He would do his work at local coffee shop or go for a quiet walk on the nearby greenway. On nights Jay threw parties that lingered into the early hours of the morning, Drew often stayed at his friend's or girlfriend's place.

Drew recalls coming home after a week-long vacation to an unrecognizable apartment. Molded, half eaten pizza still in the box, empty beer bottles scattered about, stains on his couch, but worst of all, he could tell someone had been in or stayed in his room.

Fortunately, Jay was not home at the time, because Drew's initial reaction was to "lose it." Drew notes, "I thought, 'How dare you take advantage of my kindness and patience? I have been nothing but respectful and kind to you, cleaning up after you, being cordial to your obnoxious friends. And you just step all over me!' And then it hit me...not once had I asked him to tidy up, quiet down, or uphold our agreement."

It was at that moment that Drew realized—in a sense—he had been tormenting himself. Drew states, "This whole time I was playing the victim."

This does not dismiss Jay's disregard for the house rules; but it does point out that when we tolerate bad behavior, or things we dislike, we are contributing by not doing anything about it.

Drew took a deep breath and thought about how he was going to handle the situation. When Jay arrived home, Drew decided to be honest and express how he felt about the situation.

"...Jay, I don't think you would do anything to intentionally disrespect me. That being said, I want to talk about what we agreed to when moving in together. Do you remember?"

Jay tried his best to shrug off the situation, "Yeah, I mean, I guess"—with an awkward smile and glance to the side.

"Okay, then you remember that keeping things clean and respecting each other's space was a part of that agreement?"

"Yeah, sure."

"I realize this is the first time I have mentioned this to you; mainly, because I've wanted to avoid this discussion for fear of an argument. But I am at the point where I cannot overlook it anymore. *I'm* allowing it to affect my mood and health, and I don't feel comfortable in my own home. I take full responsibility for letting it go this far without saying anything. I understand that people have different lifestyles. However, when we both agree to something, I expect us to both uphold it. Is that fair?"

"Yeah man, sorry. I just thought you didn't care and you were cool with it, since you hadn't said anything."

"And again, I take full responsibility for not saying something sooner. But going forward, I need us to be on the same page, or we will have to talk about other living arrangements. Also, I need you to find a way to get the stains off the couch."

Jay nods his head in agreement and grabs a few empty beer bottles as he makes his way to the waste basket.

Jay managed to keep his promises for three months before reverting to his old habits. Eventually, Drew had to find another roommate. However, he no longer felt anxious or uncomfortable about addressing his concerns—while still being respectful of the other person.

It's not always easy for us to accept that our tolerance can contribute to our problems. Like Drew, we can dismiss our responsibility to act or speak up; whether it's to avoid negative feelings, conflict, or facing our problems. However, we need to be aware that these forms of tolerances—and procrastination—can be a sign of low EQ.

While every situation is different, here are some steps you can take to reduce the chance of conflict and ensure you're approaching the situation with emotional intelligence:

1. Pause. Breathe. Think.
2. Take responsibility for your actions (or lack of action).
3. Remove yourself from the situation and do not take it personally.
4. View the situation from an alternative perspective.
5. Remember: Things aren't about you. Everyone has their own standards, beliefs, and ideas.
6. Find appreciation for that person and seek out your common ground.
7. Compassionately discuss your feelings, emotions and needs without judgment or criticism.

EMOTIONS CANNOT BE DESTROYED

Addressing unpleasant emotions head on can be difficult, especially if these emotions are triggered by someone you see on a frequent basis, perhaps a partner or a coworker. Sometimes it seems easier to ignore the fact that something is wrong and needs to be addressed. Many of us want to avoid conflict, unpleasant feelings, and the potential awkwardness that may follow.

We may find ourselves dropping hints through our tone of voice and body language, hoping the other party will recognize something is wrong and initiate the conversation. While others may notice something "off" about our mood, they may think we are just being difficult or cranky.

Such situations can be frustrating for all parties involved. On one hand, you have someone who is clearly upset, and on the other hand, you have someone who can see that the other person is upset but doesn't understand the cause. Rather than discussing the issue, the parties choose to sweep it under the rug and move on with their lives. However, emotions are a form of energy, and energy cannot be destroyed, only transferred. Suppressing our emotions is like squeezing the air inside a balloon; it is simply transferred to a different part of the balloon.

In 2013, the Harvard School of Public Health and the University of Rochester found that individuals who suppressed their emotions increased their risk of cancer by 70% and their risk of premature death (from all causes) by 30%.[43] Additional studies have also found that suppressed emotions correlate with high blood pressure, heart disease, diabetes, increased aggression, and mood disorders, while negatively impacting our memory and problem-solving abilities.[44] And, like a balloon, the more we squeeze, the more the pressure can build up in other areas of our life until, finally, the "balloon" bursts. Thus, an employee who gets reprimanded at work by their boss (but chooses to stay quiet so they won't lose their job) may lash out at someone else on an entirely unrelated matter. Others may resort to substance abuse to numb their pain.

Toxic emotions are like a virus that we can control or spread. They have adverse effects, can be destructive to ourselves and others, and move from person to person. And, although we have focused on toxic emotions, positive emotions can spread too. Ultimately, we have the power to decide how to manage our emotions, either as weapons or as a force for good.

10

Emotional Wildfires

"Emotions are contagious. You decide what you want to catch and what you want to spread."

— Michael J. Gelb in *The Art of Connection*

In the fall of 2007, in the rural town of Agua Dulce in Northern Los Angeles County, a young boy and a single match set 38,000 acres ablaze. As the fire raged, aided by the hot, dry weather and strong gusts of wind, 15,000 people fled their homes, over 40 buildings were destroyed, and three people were injured. It only took a spark and the right conditions to create mass devastation.

Emotions are much like wildfires; it only takes one person, sparked by strong (positive or toxic) emotions, to spread them amongst the masses. The intensity and speed at which emotion spreads is determined by every individual that encounters the "carrier" of that emotion. We can either be the wind that fans the flames, aiding in its spread, or we can choose to extinguish the emotion. In this chapter, we will learn to identify the signs of an "emotional spark" within ourselves and others, what types of emotions spread quicker than others, and how to ensure we are fueling the spread of positive emotions, while extinguishing those that are toxic.

SMOKE SIGNALS

If we take a step back and observe from afar, we will see that our landscape is dotted with the emotional smoke signals of the people all around us. Being able to recognize these signals of burning emotions within ourselves and others can help prevent toxic emotions from getting out of hand while ensuring that positive emotions continue to spread.

IDENTIFYING THE SIGNALS OF TOXIC EMOTIONS

All people handle situations and feelings in their own way. Some people respond to toxic emotions by erupting like a volcano under pressure. Others react by suppressing their emotions and retreating within themselves. Identifying the symptoms of toxic emotions residing in ourselves and others will help us to prevent them from spreading.

Identifying Toxic Emotions within Ourselves and Others

When you experience a toxic emotion inside yourself, you may:

- Feel a warm or burning sensation in your body
- Experience an increased heart rate
- Breathe fast and shallow
- Feel heaviness in your chest
- Become quick to judge or assume the worst
- Find the negative in an otherwise neutral or positive message or interaction
- Have negative thoughts about others or yourself
- Overreact

- Find it difficult to concentrate
- Find fault in yourself or others
- Experience anxiety, stress, or depression
- Have trouble sleeping or experience a lower quality of sleep
- Feel drained of energy
- Experience reduced performance on the job
- Form unhealthy habits such as binge eating, substance or alcohol abuse, or the use of physical stimulants

Toxic emotions within others may manifest as:

- Negative body language
- Snide remarks
- Unusual behavior (contrary to their usual self)
- Defensiveness or withdrawal
- Overreaction
- Hostility
- Refusal to cooperate
- Emotional outbursts
- Decreased performance
- Increased error
- Reduced tolerance
- Impatience
- Discrediting or putting down others
- Physical violence
- Verbal abuse

It can be easy to detect that something is "off" in someone we know well or spend a lot of time with. For example, a coworker who is typically warmhearted and chatty but who on this day seems to be more reserved may be feeling some form of toxic or unpleasant emotion. However, that same reserved behavior may be a neutral state for someone else. It's important for us to be aware that everyone expresses emotions differently. Some people are more easily triggered, while others seem to be immune to experiencing strong emotions.

SLOW BURN VERSUS ACCELERANT-AIDED

If you were ever in the Girl Scouts or Boy Scouts, you know there are several ways to go about creating a nice, warm, blazing fire that other troops would envy. And you were likely taught how to start that fire without a match, a lighter, or the use of accelerant, which would be considered cheating. "Fair" techniques for starting the fire include concentrating sunlight into a laser beam with a magnifying glass; striking two pieces of flint together to create a spark; or making a wood drill (creating friction between a flat piece of wood, light tinder and a stick that you vigorously rub back and forth). All these methods take time and skill, unlike the instant combustion from a lighter or match.

People and emotions work very similarly. Some people go up in flames more quickly, while others are slower to ignite and burn more gently. In other words, they are less susceptible to emotional arousal and, even when aroused, they remain in control of their emotions. For those who are easily sparked, there is hope. Through the application of emotional intelligence, we can learn to curb our emotional impulses.

NOT EVERY EMOTION IS FLAMMABLE

Not all unpleasant emotions are flammable. For example, sadness and depression are unpleasant, but they are unlikely to be projected onto others and less likely to spread. When we feel sad, lonely, or burnt out, we do not experience the increased heart rate, blood pressure, and shallow rapid breathing of our fight-or-flight response. Instead, we may feel lethargic, unmotivated, and isolated, the opposite of emotional arousal. This is because such emotions are linked to our parasympathetic nervous system, which controls homeostasis (the tendency toward stability in our physiological processes) and the digestion and rest state within our body.

Even though such emotions are less likely to spread from one person to the other, they should not go ignored and unaddressed. Emotions like sadness, loneliness, and depression need just as much attention. They can do just as much harm to the self as the more "flammable" emotions, like anger or rage. In this case, we want to spark a fire in others that can dry up their sorrow and doubts, spreading feelings of love, compassion, and understanding to those in need.

KINDNESS SET ABLAZE

Following the release of Catherine Hyde Ryan's best-selling novel *Pay It Forward* in 1999, random acts of kindness started to ignite across the United States and other countries. As the public caught wind of this phenomenon, the act of paying it forward continued to spread for years! A popular way of paying it forward started to appear at fast food drive-thrus when customers in line paid for the person in the car behind them. A notable occurrence was recorded in 2012, at a Tim Hortons in Winnipeg, Canada. An individual created a chain reaction of "paying it forward" that continued for the next 228 consecutive cars. Catherine Hyde Ryan later called this "an example of goodness gone viral." The lesson here is that the positive feeling that it generates in the giver, causes the continuation, and spread of pleasant feelings. And we don't have to spend money to "pay it forward" and make someone else's day. We might be surprised at how little it takes to change someone's current mood.

GOOD VIBES AT THE DMV

The DMV (Department of Motor Vehicles) isn't known for being the ideal place to visit if we are looking to have our spirits lifted. And too often, DMV employees are stereotyped as being loathsome people—which doesn't help matters.

While waiting in line at my local DMV, I carefully watched the interactions between the clerks and the customers—what better way to pass the time? After a handful of interactions, I noticed patterns in body language and communication between the individuals. As the clerks called the next customer over, there was about a 50/50 chance of them asking, "How are you?"; yet this was rhetorical, with little feeling behind it. Other clerks would merely call the next customer over and look up as if to say, "Tell me what I can do for you." Customer exchanges were about as unpleasant. Often, the customers were ill-prepared with the items they needed to present to the clerk. Some customers argued with the clerk about fees or late payments they claimed they were not responsible for. Throughout my observation, I tried to put myself in the position of the clerk, because many people villainize them. I wanted to switch it up and try seeing things from their perspective.

How would I feel if, day in and day out, I was dealing with people who I felt despised me, came ill-prepared, and argued with me about why they shouldn't pay their bills? As a clerk, it would be difficult to keep a positive attitude. I would find it draining to be overworked and undervalued. With that in mind, I approached the counter. I greeted the clerk with a smile and asked how her day was going. "Busy," she replied.

I handed her my paperwork—all the information and documentation I felt she needed to complete the task. I then replied, "I hope I've provided you all you need. I know your time is important and I'm sure it's frustrating when people are ill-prepared."

That is when the connection was made. She looked up as if I had unlocked a vault. "Yes. It's very frustrating. People just don't understand. I took a 15-minute lunch break today because we had people lined up around the door. It would make things run so much smoother if they came prepared."

All I did was listen to her. As she hastily took care of my needs, I complimented her on doing a great job and hoped the rest of her day was better. She replied, "It is now," with a big and genuine smile.

As I was walking away, I heard her call the next customer in line with just a little more energy and gratitude. It doesn't take much to turn someone's day around. Who knows how far one spark of positive emotion will spread?

FIGHTING FIRE WITH FIRE

A tower of brush—tree limbs, dead shrubs, hollow tree stumps—that had accumulated from the previous year's cleanup around the family land now stood eight to ten feet high. Every year in late summer or early fall (whenever we felt the stack was large enough), my grandparents and uncle hosted a bonfire with a few of their friends.

Playing with fire, especially bonfires as large as this one, can be dangerous. And when you have an uncle like mine, who thought throwing glass jars filled with gasoline onto a roaring fire was a good idea, you needed to take extra safety precautions to keep the fire from spreading or getting out of hand.

In this case, we fought fire with fire. The day before the bonfire, we created a safety perimeter by pouring and lighting a thin line of gasoline in a circle around the mound with about a 12-foot radius from the center. This way, if the fire were to spread, it would fizzle out once it reached the existing burnt perimeter. Fire needs fuel, and if you take that fuel away (in this case by pre-burning), it stays contained.

We can use these same safety precautions with our emotions and the emotions of others. We all have a responsibility not to allow our toxic moods to get out of hand and wreak havoc on those around us. It is also our responsibility to ensure we either "fireproof" ourselves from other people's emotions or try and counteract their toxic emotions with either neutral or positive emotions.

How to Manage Emotional Fires

1. **Ask yourself** *Is this an emotion worth spreading?* We want to ensure we are only putting out the toxic fires. If we are met with positivity, we don't want our potential mood (if unpleasant) to extinguish an emotion worth spreading. We also want to ensure we are not the accelerant to toxic emotions.

2. **Monitor your emotions and ensure you are handling them with care.** Ensure you are taking care of the underlying need behind the emotions to ensure toxic emotions stay self-contained.

3. **Help fight the toxic emotional fires around you.** To do this you must come from a place of understanding and compassion. Provide emotional support for others. Bring clarity to miscommunication. Counteract toxic emotions with love.

THE PHOENIX

From the ashes, the phoenix is reborn. The fires of toxic emotion can be devastating and exhausting to fight. And, because they are exhausting, they can only survive in short bursts of energy. While it may appear—based on media coverage—that we thrive on conflict, studies show that we long for positive interactions with one another and good news. The emotions connected to goodwill and kindness are not only longed for; they are empowering, contagious, and a sustainable source of energy.

Although negativity will always exist, we can choose a more wholesome and compassionate life for ourselves and generations to come. In Part III, we will learn what it takes to be a catalyst for positive change. We'll explore how to spark a new revolution in human kindness and understanding and become more emotionally intelligent beings.

PART 3

THE CATALYST FOR CHANGE

11

A New Revolution

"If we glance at the most important revolutions in history, we see at once that the greatest number of these originated in the periodical revolutions of the human mind."

— Wilhelm Humboldt

Almost every revolution begins with chaos, division, and a need for change. Humanity has reached a tipping point. We are tired of leaders who rule by fear and manipulation. We are exhausted by outrageous rants and hateful, senseless remarks. We are tired of the meaningless violence and death that result from irrational, impulsive, and extremist beliefs.

It can be overwhelming and discouraging to survey the consequences of human disunity, self-interest, and ignorance. Rather than feeling helpless, we need to ask: Where do we go from here? How do we correct our maladaptive behaviors that have been scripted by our biology and by social programming? We are always evolving in mind, body, and spirit. While our physical evolution may take many generations to observe, our minds can transform overnight, or even within a matter of seconds. The plasticity of the human mind, called *neuroplasticity*, allows us to rewire our brain by creating new neural pathways, strengthening existing pathways, and pruning the pathways we no longer need.

An analogy may help here. Let's say our brain is a snow-covered mountain. The skiers are the neurons, and their tracks are the brain's neural pathways. The more frequented the trails, the stronger the track marks (the stronger the neural connection). When skiers start to leave one trail for another—that is, when you start to break one habit to build another habit—the old trails (old habits) eventually fade and are covered by fresh snow (neural pruning).

Society works as a collective brain. Individuals are the neurons that either strengthen a collective habit/belief or break old existing habits/beliefs. Our emotions and actions are not constructed and executed in a vacuum. Rather, we need other people to shape our experiences and perceptions. From birth, we interact with others based on the feedback we receive from vocal tone, body language, and facial expression; we mimic behavior and adopt social norms. In essence, humanity is a single living organism, and human discord is a disease that can spread like cancer and destroy everything in its path.

UNLOCKING OUR FULL POTENTIAL

The scientific, technological, and digital revolutions brought with them unimaginable discoveries, advancements, and cures. Yet, so far none of these has provided a solution on how to save us from ourselves. Only a change of mind and heart can do that. This is not to say that discoveries and advancements cannot aid in understanding and developing human compassion and understanding. However, there is not a one-size-fits-all formula for developing emotional intelligence.

Scientists and philosophers have been ruminating about the human mind and heart for thousands of years. Plato (c. 427–347 BC), the ancient Greek philosopher who was a student of Socrates and a teacher to Aristotle, said that humans have a psyche (soul or consciousness). Plato describes the collective psyche as a combination of logos (logic and reasoning, located in the head and regulating the other parts of the body), thymos (emotions and spirit, which are located in the chest region), and eros (desire, which resides in the gut). Plato's idea still resonates with us today when we think about our "three brains": gut feelings, feelings of the heart, and logic of the brain.

Although we would be unable to "feel" anything without brain function, we know that our thoughts, feelings, and physical health are entangled, the result of multiple body systems working together. And, yet, we still have much to learn about the power and possibility of the unseen mind, which Aristotle (385 BC–323 BC) called "consciousness." We must tap into this consciousness to improve our emotional intelligence.

HEART FEELINGS AND BEYOND

The heart has been a symbol of emotion and love for thousands of years, beginning with Plato's theory of logos, thymos, and eros. Recent research has shown that, not only is the heart associated with love and feelings, it is perceptually linked to core human functions and values.[45]

Think of the function of your heart in relation to your emotions. When we feel anxious or upset, our heart reacts; our blood pressure rises, our heart rate increases. Toxic emotions affect the heart via heart disease, heart attacks, and hypertension. What we have always assumed to be the heart reacting to the mind is actually a two-way connection.

The HeartMath Institute (HMI), founded in 1991 by Doc Lew Childre, Jr., has built on the research first conducted in the 1960s and 70s by psychophysiology researchers John and Beatrice Lacey, regarding the ways in which the heart and the brain communicate with each other.

According to the HMI, the heart communicates with the brain and body in four ways:

- Neurologically (via the nervous system)
- Biochemically (via neurotransmitters and hormones)
- Biophysically (via pulse waves)
- Energetically (via electromagnetic fields)

Hormones and neurotransmitters, that were once only thought to be produced in the brain, have been found to also reside in the heart. In *Science of the Heart: Exploring the Role of the Heart in Human Performance*, the HMI notes, "The heart contains cells that synthesize and release catecholamines (norepinephrine, epinephrine, and dopamine), which are neurotransmitters once thought to be produced only by neurons in the brain and ganglia. More recently, it was discovered the heart also manufactures and secretes oxytocin, which can act as a neurotransmitter and commonly is referred to as the love or social bonding hormone."

Whether or not you agree that the heart is the central hub of love and compassion, we cannot deny the fact that love and compassion are the opposite of contempt and self-interest; and the latter are exactly the problems that we are trying to address.

WE YEARN FOR "GOODNESS"

We may feel distracted and bombarded by the chaos of modern life and egocentric lifestyle being pushed on us by politicians, mass media, and industries, but polls have shown that we long for goodness in the world and are more likely to repost, share, and indulge in positive, cooperative behavior than in negativity and hate.

Though all emotions are contagious, positive emotions tend to be more contagious than toxic emotions. Even though venting our frustration and anger may feel good in the moment, it ultimately does even more damage to our physical and mental state, leaving us stewing over the situation longer and flooding our bodies with chemicals that drain our energy and start the negative loop all over again. In contrast, human kindness, goodness, and compassion provide us with a flood of healthy emotions and feelings that uplift us, boost our energy levels, and motivate us to pay it forward.

While it may seem difficult to snap out of a negative feedback loop, it is much easier to do so than we might think. Psychologist Jonathan Haidt is the Thomas Cooley Professor of Ethical Leadership at New York University's Stern School of Business. In his studies of social and moral psychology, he has identified the effects of "moral elevation," the specific emotional state that an individual experiences when witnessing or hearing about the virtuous good deeds of others. After witnessing or hearing about such experiences, individuals tend to feel more optimistic about humanity, are less likely to exhibit outgroup bias, and are filled with appreciation, joy, and admiration. As Haidt writes, "The fact that we can be so responsive to the good deeds of others—even when we do not benefit directly—is a very important facet of human nature."[46]

Haidt is not the only psychologist to study the astonishing positive effects of moral elevation. Freeman, Aquino, and McFerran (2009) found that participants described the following when witnessing an act of selfless kindness: "Warmth or tingling is felt in the chest and other physical sensations." Schnall, Roper, and Fessier (2010) compared research participants' feelings of moral elevation to feelings of amusement—pleasure—on cooperative behavior.

What if we started our day by watching a video of such deeds, or recalling a moment where we witnessed an act of love and compassion? Could that be enough to spark a chain reaction of compassion within us? Based on Haidt's research, the simple answer is yes. As Haidt notes, "The effects of these feelings appear to have potentially life-altering effects. One participant described how moved he was when so many people came to visit and support his family while his grandfather was dying. He said he still had those feelings seven years later, and that those feelings helped inspire his decision to become a doctor."[47]

So, next time we are in a funk, a bad mood, or feeling glum about the state of humanity, it may be in our best interests to seek out goodness in the world. And, more importantly, put forth goodness through our own actions. Sharing an uplifting post on social media is not enough. Individuals who experience stress and depression have found that by volunteering, and selflessly giving back to the community, they are happier and more optimistic about life. When we do things for others, such as volunteering in the community, sitting with the elderly, or helping others we do not know, there is no need to document and broadcast our "good deeds" to the world. Instead, take in the experience. Notice the expressions on the faces of those you are helping. Connect with them on a deeper emotional level. Be mindful, present, and notice your change in perspective.

MINDFULNESS

The practice of mindfulness has been in existence long before many of today's major world religions were born. Although it is heavily tied to Buddhism and meditation, mindfulness is simply a state of awareness. It is our ability to bring attention to our senses and feelings of the present moment without judgment. Ask yourself: *What do I see, hear, smell, feel, and taste? What emotions am I feeling? How is my body responding to my emotions?*

Mindfulness, like any practice or belief, has its critics, who often dissect its parts without analyzing the whole. They claim that meditation and self-awareness cannot change the world. *Action*, they argue, is the primary component in the formula for change. However, while mindfulness alone may not feed the hungry, reverse climate change, or eliminate corruption, I would argue that nothing *alone* can solve any of our problems. But without mindfulness (self-awareness), it is difficult to be "still" long enough to gain an objective perspective of a situation and identify our role in the change we want to see.

In addition, mindfulness can organically evoke change within ourselves. When we become at peace with ourselves, and develop compassion for others, we begin to change how we think. This creates a constructive biochemical reaction in our brain, which then evokes positive feelings. In turn, these positive feelings promote positive behaviors and reduce stress, which correlates with increased cooperation with and understanding of others.

As we discussed earlier, emotions are contagious. By reducing our stress and anxiety and spreading a more tranquil feeling to others, we collectively begin to decrease the spread of toxic emotions which once had our bodies living in constant survival mode. This elimination of the constant feeling of fear and uncertainty reduces our urge to become defensive and opens the door to new perspectives without the need for retaliation. When we realize that entertaining new ideas will not destroy who we are, but can instead strengthen us as a collective whole, then and only then can we build a more peaceful and prosperous future for all of humanity.

THE CHICKEN OR THE EGG?

Given the unsettling fact that the vast majority of humanity currently lack self-awareness (because it is a skill that is not taught to us), where do we begin with developing emotional literacy? Who is going to teach it? The education system? Parents and guardians? Religious leaders? We can't expect people who have never been taught or developed the skill of emotional intelligence to teach others.

We also mustn't confuse guidance, manners, and moral principles with emotional intelligence. Setting boundaries, establishing guidelines, and punishing negative behavior only repress the underlying issue. Unless we are experts in human behavior, identifying and addressing the underlying causes of an individual's behavior might be a challenge. Often, we identify the symptoms and not the cause itself. In addition, because we are used to seeing the world in black and white, we may also try to identify a *single* cause when many factors combined influence individual attitudes and behaviors.

However, there is good news. We do not need to be experts in human behavior to change the world. We only need to become aware of our emotions and show compassion for ourselves and others; the rest will follow.

12

Compassion and Understanding are the Cure

"Self-absorption in all its forms kills empathy, let alone compassion. When we focus on ourselves, our world contracts as our problems and preoccupations loom large. But when we focus on others, our world expands. Our own problems drift to the periphery of the mind and so seem smaller, and we increase our capacity for connection—or compassionate action."

— Daniel Goleman, *Social Intelligence: The New Science of Human Relationships*

Compassion and empathy (a key component to emotional intelligence); the void of hatred, envy, and ego; and an unconditional understanding and love for even the most loathsome of individuals. This is the love that was preached by many of the prophets whom major religions were formed around. Jesus, Muhammad, Buddha, and Abraham all demonstrated acts of genuine kindness. And, while the act of and belief in kindness and love is so often preached, few of us embody this same wholesome compassion for our adversaries. Instead, we often resort to justification of distain for those who do not think or act in accordance with our beliefs, which leads to hypocrisy.

Others mimic compassion through acts of kindness steered by the ego. A homeless man is handed food, but not before the record button is hit on a device to say, "Look what I just did," or the story of the act is shared with others in order to receive praise and validation. If ever we (the doer) feels the need to record or share *our* selfless acts of kindness with others, we are being led by the ego.

We all have the ability within ourselves to love all of humanity but, first, we must look beyond ourselves, beyond the borders of our tribes, and the fear that may arise from not understanding our differences. As Daryl Davis—a world renowned musician and change agent—said during our interview together, "We fear what we don't know, and that fear leads to hate, and hate leads to destruction." Therefore, we must seek to understand what we do not know.

SEEKING TO UNDERSTAND

The year is 1968 and ten-year-old Daryl marches proudly, holding the American flag, as he leads his Cub Scout troop on a march from Lexington to Concord, MA, in commemoration of the ride of Paul Revere. Suddenly, Daryl is being hit with debris—bottles, rocks, and cans—that are being flung by a group of spectators. Daryl assumes the angry crowd doesn't like the scouts, until troop leaders surround Daryl and escort him to safety. That's when he realizes it isn't the scouts they are targeting, it's him, a black boy, ignorant to the hatred of racism.

However, Daryl did not let the hatred of others transform into bitterness. Instead, he sought to objectively answer one question: "How can you hate me, when you don't even know me?" As an adult, Daryl reflects back to the incident and says, "It was inconceivable to me that someone who had never laid eyes on me, never spoken to me, knew absolutely nothing about me, would want to inflict pain upon me for no other reason... than the color of my skin."

Daryl Davis is an international musician, who has played with legends like B.B King, Jerry Lewis, and Chuck Berry; and has no formal background in psychology or sociology. Yet, he has been the catalyst for over 200 members of the KKK (Ku Klux Klan) to leave the klan and denounce hatred and racism. Not because he tried to convince them that they were wrong. Instead, Daryl's genuine desire to understand and come from a place of compassion is the catalyst for change.

Shortly after the incident in 1968, Daryl began to read books about racism, white supremacy, the KKK, and neo-Nazism, to gain a better understanding of their beliefs and where this hatred stems from. Once Daryl reached adulthood, he began to meet with members of the KKK, and attend their rallies as an observer. Daryl states, "I would try to absorb and understand, not that I'm believing in what they're preaching, but I am trying to learn to understand what the impetus for it is. Racism is something that is learned; and if it can be learned, it can be unlearned."

The first time Daryl asked "how can you hate me when you don't even know me?" he received responses like blacks are criminals, based on the fact there are more blacks in prison than whites; blacks are lazy and live off of welfare; blacks have smaller brains and are an inferior race.

Instead of responding with rage to the offensive remarks, Daryl let them "get it all out" he says. Daryl calmly and respectfully assured the klan members that he had never been in trouble with the law, never been on welfare, and while he had never measured his brain, he was sure it was no smaller than anyone else's.

What makes Daryl's story so remarkable is his ability to not take their ignorance as a personal attack. What would make most of us want to fire back with insults, rage and furry, Daryl saw as an opportunity to educate and enlighten.

Not once did he try to convince them they were wrong. The change occurred organically. It was his willingness to understand and show compassion in the face of adversity that subsequently opened the hearts and minds of his adversaries. Before Daryl speaks, he listens without interruption. "Respect is key," Daryl says. And it takes time. Some klansmen took years to leave the klan and change their ways of thinking. One of which was Grand Dragon (state leader of the klan), Roger Kelly. Even after several years of knowing and admittingly respecting Daryl, Kelly stated during a CNN interview back in 1996, "It hasn't changed my views about the klan you know, because my views about the klan has been pretty much cemented in my mind for years."

It took two additional years after this interview for Roger to denounce his affiliation with the klan and apologize for his misguided beliefs and hateful acts. Finally, Daryl remarks at the closing of his TEDxNaperville Talk, "If I can do that [referring to his willingness to listen and understand] anybody in here can do that."

SELF-COMPASSION FIRST

It's difficult—if not impossible—for us to show compassion for others if we have yet to show it for ourselves. We often beat ourselves up when we do not achieve the (often unrealistic) expectations we set, or the expectations we believe are being set for us by others. We are a competitive society that awards people for being the "best", focusing on comparisons, instead of awarding on individual merit and progress. We are encouraged to compare our skill sets, intelligence, looks, and possessions against others. When we fall short, we may feel many unpleasant emotions like anger, denial, envy, and sadness. These comparisons, driven by the ego, can smother self-love and appreciation.

Self-compassion and appreciation should not be mistaken for narcissism which is an unrealistic and exaggerated perception of the importance of the self. Self-compassion, in contrast, is a genuine appreciation and acceptance for who we are, flaws and all. While we will never be perfect, if we strive to become our best self—absent of excuses, and justifications for our poor behavior—we will live much more fulfilling lives. And, once we have accepted ourselves for who we truly are, we can then radiate that same appreciation and acceptance for others.

How to develop self-compassion:
1. Humble yourself. Acknowledge your imperfections.
2. Realize that being "the best" at something is an illusion.
3. Only compare yourself to yourself.
4. Set SMART goals for yourself: Specific, Measurable, Attainable, Realistic, and Time-bound.
5. Acknowledge incremental progress.
6. Be understanding when you do not meet your expectations. Have a "try, try again" mentality. Remember, Rome wasn't built in a day.
7. Repeat steps 1-6.

ACCEPTING OTHERS FOR WHO THEY ARE

With perfection seeming to be our subconscious social standard for one another, it is easy to overlook the beauty and value that lies within every human being. It's tough for others to know when we are projecting our insecurities onto them, and it's even harder for them to come from a place of understanding when they believe they are under attack.

Once we find compassion, we see even the most despised individuals through a different lens. We notice the conditioning that led to the harsh words, negative actions, and the mistakes they are making in their lives.

Being one of those people who could be hateful, talking down to and about others, I now realize I was coming from a place of self-hate. It had little (and sometimes nothing) to do with the people on the receiving end.

Compassion starts with taking responsibility. It means checking ourselves to prevent projection of our frustrations onto others. It is just as important, when we are facing the wrath of others, that we view the attackers with genuine compassion instead of taking their words as a personal attack.

Genuine compassion is not pity, sarcasm, or self-congratulatory. How many times have you heard people say, "You know, I feel sorry for you. I really do," or "You need help. I'll pray for you," with a condescending undertone, or "I'm going to be the 'bigger' person here"? These statements do not express genuine compassion. Instead, they are often conveyed with an air of contempt.

True compassion does not need to be stated and defined as such. Genuine care and understanding can take the form of a listening ear, a soft smile of forgiveness, the willingness to walk away, or an offer of support. Those whom we see as evil, as villains, are people who feel broken inside and who need our love and support. When we can feel compassion for villains, we will begin to see true change in this world.

What stops most people from displaying compassion for others is the belief that certain people don't deserve compassion. These misguided beliefs stem from our ego; we exalt ourselves and dismiss our own shortcomings when we judge others.

Showing compassion does not mean we have to take what others are dishing out; nor does it imply we agree with their behavior. We can still stand up for ourselves and what we believe to be just and moral, set boundaries, choose to walk away, and be assertive. It's those difficult moments, when stress is at an all-time high, that put your ability to choose compassion and understanding over contempt to the test.

Choosing Selfless Understanding

After eight years together, Holly and John decided to separate. It was clear their lives were going in different directions. Holly was tired of feeling alone and lacking a true partner in life. The relationship felt one-sided.

John felt Holly was controlling and bossy, and he became curious about seeing other people. The day finally came when they both realized they needed to take a break, have some time apart, and figure out what they really wanted.

Early into the separation, Holly realized she was ready to move on with her life, without him. While she still cared about John, she knew their lives were too different to make it work. They had grown too far apart and were different people than they were eight years ago.

Soon, John was dating Katie, a woman they both went to high school with. Holly happened to run into Katie a few months prior to the separation. They had a friendly chat and caught up on life. Katie went on to say what a "cute couple" Holly and John made, and the two ladies continued to have friendly conversation over Facebook. However, once Katie began to date John, things changed.

Two months into their relationship—a mere four months into Holly and John's separation, John announced Katie was expecting. Holly was both shocked and hurt. One of their main arguments was regarding children. Holly was ready and John had no desire to be a father. Although the two were separated, they continued to talk, and Holly stayed close to John's family. John began to share his concerns about the situation with her, saying he didn't intend to be a father and he felt Katie was using it as a "trap". He felt Katie seemed to have an unhealthy obsession with "competing" with Holly. As things began to escalate, Holly distanced herself from John and his family to keep the peace.

One month later, Holly receives a call from John's aunt, whom she was close with. She asked if Holly had heard the news. John had been in a near-fatal car accident. She informed Holly, "The report showed he was speeding, it was raining, and he lost control of the car, hitting a telephone pole head on. Doctors are not sure if he's going to survive. He's in a coma, with multiple broken bones and both lungs punctured."

While he and Holly were not together, she was still his wife and, was appalled that no one had made the effort to contact her. But then Holly stepped back and looked at the big picture. Here is a family who might lose their son. Their last concern is whether they should contact his soon to be ex-wife. In addition, Katie was claiming she might miscarry if Holly came to the hospital; that it would "put too much stress on her and the baby."

Seeing that the family had enough to worry about without additional drama, Holly decided not to go to the hospital and instead kept up-to-date through John's aunt.

Holly recalls, "I was a bit torn on what to do. I thought, maybe I should reach out and let her know I'm not a threat, that I only want to see them happy. And I did. I know the feelings of insecurity she was experiencing. I had been there myself at times. So, I reached out."

Unfortunately, Holly's sincere attempts to connect and offer support were met with bitter hatred, name calling, and physical threats from Katie.

"Later, when I went to gather my things from our home (Holly and John's home), I found that my wedding dress from the storage shed was gone. I can only imagine she dumped it. In addition, many of my personal belongings were ransacked and destroyed. Many family heirlooms and childhood toys. I was devastated, angry; I wanted to file charges. And, looking back, maybe I should have. But it wouldn't bring them back," Holly notes.

Holly said the only thing that kept her from feeling a lifetime of resentment for Katie was empathy. She understood that, while her acts appeared to be a personal attack, there was something deeper at play.

Finally, Holly says, "We cannot choose how people will react to our willingness to help and come from a place of understanding. But we can choose how we will handle it. While many view Katie as a 'crazy bitch,' I see someone who needs love and understanding. While the things she both said and did were uncalled for, there is something deeper she is feeling."

Katie, like many who are emotionally disturbed, are often living in constant "survival mode." While we are each responsible for ourselves, sometimes it takes someone from the outside to not see us as a villain, but as a human in need, before we can see the light in ourselves.

"Love and compassion are necessities, not luxuries. Without them humanity cannot survive."

—Dalai Lama

13

De-villainizing the Villain

"There are no 'good' or 'bad' people. Some are a little better or a little worse, but all are activated more by misunderstanding than malice."

— **Tennessee Williams**

Disliking a villain is easy, because our definition of villains is clear: They are mean and nasty, and they hurt others, physically and emotionally.

As you sit in a crowded movie theater filled with children, you can hear cheering as the villain is defeated. The "good guys" win most of the time. This portrayal of "good" verses "bad" may be viewed as a positive, teaching children to emulate the hero. If they choose to be a bad guy, they will have to face the negative consequences. No one likes a bad guy.

A few storytellers have taken a different approach, showing the villain's human side. Dr. Seuss's character, The Grinch, is an excellent example. If you are unfamiliar with the story, here is a quick recap: The Grinch is a green creature, a "Who"—as the residents are called—who isn't very nice. He lives in lonely isolation—with only his loyal dog Max for companionship—at the top of the steep and snowy Mount Crumpit, which overlooks the village of Whoville.

In the 2000, Universal Pictures version of *The Grinch Stole Christmas*, the story is a bit more complicated:

The Grinch is an angry "Who," who terrorizes the other Whos of Whoville. He sneaks down to their town, steals their Christmas gifts, and wreaks havoc. No one likes the Grinch. Then, one day, Cindy Lou Who meets the Grinch face-to-face at her father's post office.

Cindy Lou, saved by the Grinch, sees something in him that no one else does: a softer side. Curious, Cindy Lou sets off to learn about the Grinch's past. She learns that he came to Whoville as a baby and was adopted by elderly sisters. As a young boy, the Grinch loved Christmas and created a special gift for his school crush, Martha May Whovier. A bully named Augustus May Who did not like the fact that "his girl" had taken a liking to the Grinch. So, Augustus proceeded to mock and ridicule him.

As the Grinch became the laughingstock of Whoville, he found comfort in isolation and developed a hardened heart; unleashing his nasty feelings and behaviors against the people of Whoville. Only after he receives empathy and compassion from little Cindy Lou Who, did the Grinch open his heart again, revealing the softer and kinder side of the young boy he once was.

FEELINGS FOR THE "VILLAINS"

Many of us can relate to the Grinch's story. There are so many misunderstood people in this world, people who have been an outcast, a laughingstock, a victim of bullying or abuse. Such people can protect themselves by developing a hardened heart. Like the people of *Whoville*, many of us will not take the time to learn about their struggles or show empathy for them. However, only when we make the effort to come from a place of pure compassionate understanding can we soften and mend the hardened hearts of the misunderstood.

Megamind is another great example of a misunderstood villain. Unlike the Grinch (whose negative experience influenced his behavior), Megamind was sent to Earth as a baby in a capsule at the same time as another superpower baby named Goody Two Shoes. However, Megamind's capsule landed in a prison yard, while Goody Two Shoes' capsule ended up at the doorstep of a wealthy family. Megamind, raised in a prison and parented by prisoners, learned to be good at being bad, growing up to be a super villain. Meanwhile, Mr. Goody Two Shoes became a superhero.

This movie is a beautiful demonstration of how our environments have a major influence on how we think and behave and how others view us. This can often be the case for at risk youth. Their parents do not have a "villain" gene. They are not intrinsically bad people. Instead, they have adopted behaviors that are supported and reinforced by their environment.

A core belief in the United States is that people can have whatever they want if they do the necessary work. Indeed, this is often the definition of the American Dream. However, there are individuals who have a severe disadvantage and must put in many times the work to achieve the same results as others. Not to mention the toxic environments (mental and physical) they may live in; resource deficits; and battling stigmas, all of which they must overcome. This can lead to a feeling of helplessness and cause some individuals to resort to unlawful behaviors, while being labeled a "villain" by many in society.

There are several reasons why people might be viewed as a "villain." Environment, conditioning, self-protection, desperation, and fear can lead the best of us to behave in ways we otherwise wouldn't. When we can identify their motivations and experiences, we can see past their words and actions and, in doing so, we begin to see them as human beings in need and not as evil villains.

It is difficult to dislike someone when we know their entire story. However, we don't always have the luxury or the time to get to know everyone's story. By understanding what influences "villainous" behaviors, we can begin to approach these misunderstood individuals with compassion and understanding and identify and control the villain that lies within ourselves.

THE SOCIOECONOMIC VILLAIN

Socioeconomic status (SES) depends on a combination of variables, including income, education, occupation, wealth, and residential environment. Our SES is a strong predictor of our quality of life and our ease of access to opportunities and privileges in our society. Individuals born to a low SES family are at an unfair disadvantage.

They are more likely to have greater stressors and to encounter more and higher obstacles throughout their life. Numerous studies have found low SES correlates with higher levels of stress, anxiety, and depression; emotional and behavior difficulties; delinquent behavior; suicide attempts; substance abuse; hostility; criminal activity; and symptoms related to ADHD (lack of restraint, mood swings, hyperactivity, aggression, difficulty focusing, and impulsivity).[48] These symptoms do exist in the lives of those with high SES, but they are far more prevalent in low SES individuals.

These symptoms can conjure toxic emotions. And when people bathe in toxic emotions, they are less likely to think rationally, more likely to perceive others as a threat (because they are living in survival mode), and to act on emotional impulses.

Is it any wonder that a large population of low-SES adolescents find themselves with a criminal record before reaching adulthood? These are not intrinsically "bad" children. They are children, adolescents and adults who often don't know any other life and do not feel they have other options.

177

These individuals need support from their community and civil servants. This might include policies that support upward mobility; at-risk youth programs that offer mentorship, support, resources, and guidance; and strong relationships with law enforcement and the criminal justice system. It takes a village to catalyze change for these individuals.

THE NURTURED VILLAIN

On the playground at the elementary school stood a small crowd gathered around an aluminum slide. Two boys caught a toad and one of them was holding it up by its little leg.

A young onlooker screamed, pleading for them to let the little toad go, but the two boys just laughed. The toad's frail body, released from the boy's grasp, slammed onto the metal slide. The other boy lifts his foot, smashing it down and crushing the innocent creature.

Based on the actions of these two boys, we might assume they are cruel and heartless children. However, their upbringing may have a major influence on the way they view the world and its creatures. If they were raised not to have equal respect for all living things, their action was likely a learned behavior.

Trying to bring awareness to these individuals can be difficult and sometimes impossible. Adopted and learned beliefs are unlikely to change without the willingness of the "believer" to embrace or seek alternative perspectives. Toxic nurtured beliefs often revolve around prejudices such as racism and sexism. These individuals are often taught to see others they stereotype as a threat to them or their beliefs. This underlying fear, gone unaddressed and uncorrected, can lead to hate regardless of whether they've had a personal negative experience or interaction.

Positive experiences, interactions, and exposure is one of the best ways to open the hearts and minds of these individuals. Telling them they are wrong will only strengthen their preexisting beliefs. It is best to approach them with curiosity instead of judgment, with compassion instead of resentment—as Daryl Davis did and continues to do.

THE SELF-PROTECTIVE VILLAIN

Self-protective villains feel the need to protect themselves by becoming proactively defensive. For example, they might talk negatively about people whom they envy, or lash out at those who they feel are judging them. Essentially, they create a self-fulfilling prophecy, causing people to react to them in exactly the negative ways they anticipated.

Such behavior, while ultimately dysfunctional, is understandable. If the stresses and the pressures of the outside world—or those we have created in our mind—become too much to bear or make us feel threatened, our survival instinct can be triggered. When our body goes into survival mode, our nature is to self-protect, initiating defensiveness and guiding us to respond to others with hostile behaviors or words.

Self-protective villains are highly responsive to compassion and understanding. However, this is not a response they often receive. When we are on the receiving end of their attacks, it's difficult for us to not take it personally. We have to be conscious of their need to be understood and not take their projection of insecurity personally. If you notice someone who is exhibiting "self-protective villain" behavior, acknowledge their emotions and allow for clarification.

For example, you might say:

"By the tone of your voice, I am picking up on some strong emotions. Would you mind telling me what you are feeling?"

If you feel they are projecting their emotions onto you, for example, they might say:

"You are a worthless human being and what is wrong with the world today!"

This comment can cause many negative emotions and feelings to arise within us, due to the attack on our character. Here is where we must check in with ourselves, see past the words, and stay objective and rational. You might respond with:

"When you say I am 'a worthless human being and what is wrong with the world today,' I feel attacked and angry. I'm also concerned and would like to ask what I have done to make you feel so negatively about me."

You have addressed two things: (1) How you feel about being attacked and (2) acknowledging their remarks.

Conversations like these can go back and forth. However, I have found that, if I stay objective and calm, the other person almost always comes around. It may not be at that moment; it may even take days or weeks for them to apologize or acknowledge their behavior. If you feel the conversation is simply going in circles and you notice your ability to stay objective is waning, it is best to calmly end or postpone the conversation. You can do this by stating:

"I'm finding it hard to control my emotions and stay objective. I think it may be best for us to step away until I can collect my thoughts and calm down."

Taking responsibility in moments when we are the one under attack takes humility and strength. At the same time (whether they admit it or not), it also earns you respect from the antagonist and will likely make the follow-up conversation more productive. After all, the self-protective villain is only a villain when they feel under attack. By you providing a safe place for discussion, you are already having a positive effect on their behavior.

THE DESPERATE VILLAIN

Have you been in conversation with someone and tried desperately to get your point across, but you do not feel the other person is truly hearing you? Even worse, that person may mock you, tell you they understand when they clearly do not, or say they are listening when they are simply waiting for their turn to speak.

When we are desperate to be understood, desperate to have a need met, our inner villain can come out. We may believe it's the only way to be heard. Sometimes it's a cry for help that is masked by nasty, hateful words and, in extreme cases, violence. Often, the intensity of the words, and the force behind our words or actions, indicates the level of pain or angst someone is feeling. What "desperate villains" need most is a nonjudgmental ear.

I'm sure we all know what it's like to feel the frustration that comes with being misunderstood. When met with these emotions from another, remember what it felt like when you were in their position. Ask yourself: *What might I be doing to make them feel unheard or misunderstood?* If someone tells us, "You don't understand!" we need to humbly acknowledge that we are missing something in their message. Without interruption or correction, we must listen to what they have to say—even if we do not necessarily agree with them. The goal of conversation should be to understand, not to prove a point. To ensure we are clearly receiving the message, try paraphrasing what you think you hear them saying. If they correct you, identify the potential disconnect that may be creating a gap in communication. Letting our personal opinions, beliefs, or experiences influence our interpretation of their message can cause frustration and hinder progress in conversations.

Labeling people as villains can be dehumanizing. For those doing the labeling, such labels can help them justify their lack of empathy and their unwillingness to help, reducing their cognitive dissonance. For those being labeled, the labeling can create feelings of isolation and unworthiness, much like the Grinch felt. As a result, they may become more "villainous" than they were before, out of pure hopelessness.

Therefore, it is important for us to be able to recognize these traits in ourselves and in others and detach ourselves from the situation. Often, hateful worlds and actions are a projection of the self.

PROJECTION

Psychological projection occurs when we have unpleasant feelings or emotions within or about ourselves and project them onto someone else. It is a common subconscious defense mechanism used to cope with or avoid addressing these emotions.

When we are on the receiving end of someone's projection, a frequent reaction is to assume we are being personally attacked and become defensive. If we aren't careful, projections of personal insecurity can lead to confrontation, with an exchange of unpleasant and hurtful words from all parties involved, and a potential loss of relationships or business.

A Failed Collaboration

It's not uncommon for solopreneurs to collaborate with other business professionals whose services complement their own. Julianna and Mark were both independent business owners who focused on aiding small to medium-sized businesses around human resources. Julianna focused heavily on training and development, while Mark specialized in compensation, policy, and employee handbooks. Following their introduction through a mutual connection, the two decided to meet for coffee at a local Starbucks. The initial meeting was promising, and Julianna and Mark decided to give collaboration a try.

However, shortly after pursuing their first client, some clashes in their approach became apparent. Julianna noticed Mark had an unhealthy interest in his competition, stating many times, "We can't lose this one. I've heard through the grapevine that XYZ company may be trying to steal them from us."
Julianna—who went through sales training—was always taught, "You can't lose what you don't already have." Yet Mark, eager to win the client, seemed more interested in giving his services away than in convincing them of the value he would bring in the long term. Julianna, on the other hand, preferred to start with a higher bid and itemize services in accordance with cost. It became apparent that Julianna and Mark were on two different pages when it came to business strategy and service value.

Less than a week into their collaboration, Mark asked if Julianna would handle meetings and follow-ups with the prospect while he attended to a personal matter. Julianna was happy to oblige, understanding that life happens, and the show must go on.

While constructing the proposal together, red flags began to arise for Julianna. Mark, approximately 20 years Julianna's senior, would frequently point out her lack of experience compared to his own. Although he often asked for her input and feedback, if it wasn't in alignment with what he wanted to hear it was instantly dismissed with a condescending laugh and a reminder of his 25 years of experience. Julianna was told on multiple occasions that her ideas were "ridiculous", followed by more condescending laughter and, "Give me a break, Julianna!" This continued for a few weeks until (inevitably) things came crashing down.

Mark was suddenly impatient to talk to the prospective client as he felt "out of the loop," despite the fact that he'd made himself absent for many of the scheduled calls and follow-ups. When the client responded that they had a full plate and no time to jump on a call, instead of being understanding, he became highly defensive, stating he, "Didn't want to work with someone who couldn't make time for him."

Julianna assured Mark it was not personal. However, she was both irritated and confused at his eagerness to reject the client and disengage, while professing such a strong desire to win the business. Julianna mentioned the contradiction to Mark, noting: "But I thought you said we couldn't afford to lose this one?"

He snapped. Mark then proceeded to tell Julianna that she was "condescending," "a know-it-all who knows nothing", and a "junior, mediocre trainer at best" (although Mark had never witnessed her trainings). He raged that she needed to "have respect for people with more experience" than herself, calling her "a bully" that was "railroading him."

While everything inside her wanted to defend herself, Julianna noticed that many of the accusations were a direct reflection of Mark's *own* behaviors and actions while they had been working together. Instead, she stayed calm, trying her best to empathize, stating, "I am sorry to hear you feel that way Mark. Would you mind telling me what I have said or done that has made you feel [X]?" Instead of giving examples, Mark responded with laughter, "See! You are doing it now! You're being condescending!"

Julianna knew the conversation was not going in a productive direction. It was simply a broken record of Mark projecting his feelings and emotions onto her and, while she was empathetic to his situation, she wasn't going to take his verbal abuse. Politely, she told him that because they were not engaging in a productive conversation, she was going to end the call.

Later that evening, Mark sent Julianna an apology, explaining that he had a lot going on in his life and had been under tremendous stress. Because of this, he felt the need to vent and direct his frustration at someone else. While Julianna was understanding, she made it clear that his directing emotions at her—someone who was there to help—was unacceptable and he was not someone she was willing to collaborate with anymore.

Like Julianna, we can show compassion and understanding, remain calm, and empathize. We do not have to be run over by the emotional instability that others project onto us. Julianna was able to detach herself from Mark's emotions and acknowledge that they were being projected onto her. Having this awareness allowed Julianna not to take it personally, which made it easier for her to focus on the underlying reasons for Marks behavior and words.

When we can observe our toxic interactions with others objectively, we begin to see a different side of these individuals. We may see individuals who are hurting, lost, confused, and unable to cope with their emotions. This is when we begin to de-villainize the villain and potentially start to reveal the villain within ourselves.

IDENTIFYING THE VILLAIN INSIDE OURSELVES

Identifying how we address other people and feel about others is often a good indication of how we view ourselves. We have all been a villain at some point in our lives, even if it was only for a split second when we unfairly lashed out during a moment of panic and stress.

Of the villain types that we discussed, which ones have you recognized within yourself?

_____

_____

_____

_____

_____

What were the circumstances you reacted to?

_____

_____

_____

_____

_____

_____

_____

What were you feeling at the time?

_____

_____

_____

_____

Which of your responses or actions made you feel like a "villain"?

_____

_____

_____

_____

How did others receive your reaction or response?

_____

_____

_____

_____

_____

How did their response make you feel?

_____

_____

_____

_____

_____

Looking back, what would you have done differently?

_____

_____

_____

_____

_____

_____

_____

_____

_____

Behind hateful words and actions, there is always a hidden message. The question is: Are we willing to find it?

14

The Hidden Message

"Our words are often only vague, inadequate descriptions of our thoughts. Something gets lost in translation every time we try to express our thoughts in words. And when the other person hears our words, something gets lost in translation again, because words mean different things to different people. "

— **Oliver Gaspirtz**

Emotional intelligence and effective communication go hand in hand. It takes all the elements of EQ to be responsible for the messages we are conveying and sensitive to the messages we are interpreting. Equally important, we must have the ability to self-regulate and control the feelings that may arise from hearing a message that may not be easy or pleasant to receive.

Communication is one of the most powerful tools we have. It's how we connect with each other, build relationships, create and solve problems. Our communication can start and end wars, mend broken hearts, and save lives. For us to use this powerful tool every day of our lives but not have been taught how to use it effectively, is like leaving a young child to fend for themselves. A lot of things could go wrong.

Being an effective communicator takes skill and patience. Not only do we need to ensure we properly convey what we are really feeling, we also have to be able to detect the messages of others through the noise of their emotions. Simultaneously, we have to keep in constant check with ourselves. When you are communicating, ask yourself:

- *What am I feeling?*
- *What might I be conveying as absolute truths that are simply my opinions and personal beliefs?*
- *Am I being open to what they have to say, or am I stuck in my own head?*
- *Is my message clear, or am I leaving out key details that my listener will fill in, perhaps inaccurately?*

While we are checking in with ourselves, we must also be able to turn down our inner voice so we can hear what the other person is trying to communicate. To do so, we can ask questions such as:

- *Does their tone and body language match their words?*
- *What emotions am I picking up from them?*
- *What emotions am I feeling while they are communicating?*
- *Am I letting my emotions get in the way of me hearing their message?*
- *Is what they are saying personal, or are they projecting onto me?*
- *What is the potential underlying message here?*
- *Am I approaching the conversation with compassion and genuine understanding, or with defensiveness, contempt, and hostility?*

Being an effective communicator is like being a detective. We must look at all the clues that people are giving us and not allow our own opinions to get in the way of the facts. In this chapter, we will look at what often goes overlooked and unchecked in how we convey and interpret messages. At the end, you will have the tools you need to construct a solid and objective message and a "third eye" for communication, with the ability to see beyond the words that someone uses.

SWISS CHEESE COMMUNICATION

Swiss cheese and communication have a lot in common. Like Swiss cheese, our messages are not always solid; there are a lot of holes. However, we do not like holes in our communication, so, if someone presents a message with holes in it, we will fill in the gaps for ourselves. Assumptions and miscommunications are often borne of us filling in the missing information.

Being able to identify what is missing in our communication takes skill and practice. We not only try to fill the "holes" in other people's messages, we also attempt to fill the possible "holes" in our own message before we speak. However, it's rare that the full thought comes out into words.

As an example, consider communicating the instructions for making a peanut butter and jelly (PB&J) sandwich.

If I asked you to write instructions on how to make a PB&J sandwich, you would probably feel confident about it. You were probably making PB&Js while you were still in grade school, so this task should be a no-brainer. However, I have used this exercise in communication workshops, and very few people were able to write a complete set of directions without gaps. Often, instructions end up looking something like this:

1. *Get two slices of bread.*
2. *Spread the peanut butter onto one slice of bread.*
3. *Spread the jelly on the other slice of bread.*
4. *Put them together.*
5. *Eat.*

Sounds clear, right? But now imagine that you have never made a sandwich before (in particular a PB&J). You will see that the instructions have many "holes" left to fill. Let's now plug those holes with a set of complete instructions.

You will need a bag of sliced bread, a jar of jelly, a jar of peanut butter, a butter knife, and a plate (optional).

1. *First, open the bag of bread and take out two slices. Place them side by side on a plate or table.*
2. *Open both the jar of jelly and peanut butter (you may need to twist or lift the lid off and peel off the protective material first).*
3. *Take the butter knife and scoop out about two tablespoons of peanut butter (use your judgment); now spread the peanut butter across one side of one slice of bread, evenly.*
4. *Clean the knife (however you so choose).*
5. *Now, use the knife to scoop out about one or two tablespoons of jelly and spread on the second slice of bread in the same manner as you did with the peanut butter.*
6. *Set down the knife and carefully pick up both slices of bread (one in each hand) from the bottom where there is no jelly or peanut butter.*
7. *Place the two slices of bread together so that the peanut butter and the jelly are facing one another, ensuring the edges of the bread line up.*
8. *Eat and enjoy!*

Were the individuals who wrote the first set of instructions clueless on how to make a PB&J sandwich? Not at all. Take a moment to think how simple it is to make a PB&J sandwich. If we can fail in communicating the steps in such a simple process, how are we communicating things that are more important or complex?

DEVELOPING A STRONG FOUNDATION FOR COMMUNICATION

Self-awareness is the foundation on which emotional intelligence is built. If the foundation is not solid, everything else will fail.

Developing self-awareness is a process that combines introspection with soliciting feedback from others. In terms of communication, here are some questions you might ask yourself:

- *Do I often feel my message is being understood?*
- *What are common emotions I feel when communicating with others?*
- *How do others usually receive my messages?*
- *What common feedback do I receive from others regarding my communication style?*

If we often feel our message is being misinterpreted, it could very well be that we are providing our listener with "Swiss cheese" communication. Like the PB&J instructions, not everything is being conveyed. In addition, we may be conveying the *wrong* message. Let's look at a common scenario regarding ineffective communication.

Getting to the Heart of the Matter

Blair continuously asks his roommate, Chris, not to leave his clothes lying around the house. Blair feels that his requests are falling on deaf ears. One day, when Chris gets home, Blair yells out, "You do nothing around this house to help me! All I've asked is for you to pick up your clothes and you can't even do that! You are lazy!"

To Chris, the only thing being communicated is disgust, sprinkled with insults. Unless Chris is an effective communicator, he is likely to miss the hidden message behind Blair's emotions and become defensive.

Like Blair, we can allow our emotions to build up and create a negative narrative inside our heads, based purely on our interpretation of others' actions and words. Our internal dialogue can get out of control, as we mull over situations and build on them over time. Eventually, we release our pent-up emotions on others.

When we communicate, we need to be cognizant of several factors:

- Our emotions and feelings.
- The needs behind our emotions.
- How we will convey our needs.
- The perspective of the listener or "receiver."

Let's walk through each of these points from Blair's perspective.

1. What are the emotions that Blair might be feeling?
At first, Blair probably feels annoyed, unappreciated, irritated, and frustrated. These emotions could turn into anger, bitterness, disgust, or contempt as time goes on. When we have these unpleasant feelings, it is often because a need is not being met.

2. What needs might Blair feel are not being met?
- A need to live in a clutter-free environment.
- A need to feel heard.
- A need to feel respected.

Unfortunately, Blair's message did not convey these needs. Instead, he communicated only his emotions.

3. How can Blair better convey his message?

While Blair's roommate, Chris, may not care about living in a mess, he may not be doing it out of spite. However, spite can be the result if Chris believes that Blair is speaking to him in a way that belittles him or makes him feel like a child. Let's now revise the message to reflect Blair's feelings and needs while also being aware of Chris's perspective.

Blair: "Chris, I value our friendship, and there was obviously a reason we decided to live together. I don't want to make you feel as though you still live at home with your parents by constantly asking you to pick up your belongings. However, that's how I feel sometimes. On good days, I feel annoyed. On days like today, when I've been under high stress, seeing your belongings scattered around I feel bitter toward you, disgusted, and angry. I don't want to feel that way. I really need to know that you care about our friendship enough to acknowledge my frustration and put in the effort to keep the common area clean. Is what I'm asking a reasonable request?"

While this might seem like a mouthful, the message is clear and effective, with no holes. Here, Blair carefully constructs a message that explains the situation, how it makes him feel, and his needs, while showing empathy for Chris by pointing out how constantly asking him to clean up might make him feel.

IT'S ALL IN <u>HOW</u> YOU SAY IT

A few of my clients have told me that they've tried the above approach, yet it hasn't worked out for them. My question is always: *How* did you say it? Words account for only approximately 7% of the message that is being delivered. The remaining 93% is a combination of tone and body language.[49] For example, sarcasm (reflected in tone as well as body language) can kill productive communication and be counterproductive to your desired outcome.

Put yourself on the defensive end of a difficult conversation. When someone speaks to you in a sarcastic or accusatory tone, are you more likely to be understanding and helpful, or are you more likely to do everything in your power to antagonize them? Many of us instinctually want to push back. "How dare they disrespect me? Who do they think they are? I will show them!" may be a few of the thoughts that run through our minds.

To communicate effectively, it takes energy to empathize and develop a constructive and well-received message.

As an example, let's look at an excerpt from the popular reality show *The Real World.* See if you can identify the meanings and feelings behind the message between Julie and her father in episode one, season one.

The Real World (first season, episode one):

The introduction to *The Real World* with a compilation of the cast saying: *"This is the true story... of seven strangers picked to live in a loft and have their lives taped to find out what happens when people stop being polite ... and start getting real. The real world."*

One of the seven cast members is Julie, a 19-year-old from Birmingham, Alabama. Julie wants to follow her passion for dance, but her father wants her to become a computer operator. One of the first scenes takes place in the kitchen, where Julie and her father are standing with people who appear to be members of their family.

Dad: *Well, smile Julie.*

Julie: *I'm not real happy.*

Dad: *Durn if you don't look happy.*

Julie: *I don't know, I don't think you realize you're not going to see me for a while.*

... the show cuts to a scene from Julie's perspective (in the back seat of the car) of her dad driving her to the airport, saying final goodbyes, and Julie on the plane looking out the window as if reflecting on the events that unfolded earlier that day. Now, back in the kitchen, it's as if the conversation picked up where it left off with Julie and her father.

Dad: *Well, don't you think we think alike?*

Julie: *No, I don't at all.*

Dad: *Well, where do we differ? Well, I'd probably like to know.*

Julie: *Where do we differ?*

Dad: *Yes.*

Julie: (smiling) *I think that it's okay to wear whatever you want to wear ... and not cut your hair... whereas you don't think that's okay.*

Dad: *... [G]o ahead, what else is it that you don't like about me?*

Julie: *I hate it that it took these people getting here [MTV camera crew] to make you listen to what anyone else has to say about anything. I just think it's very evident in the way that we think that there's a big age difference.*

Dad: *I, ugh, I still care about you honey. Did you know it?*

Julie: *Well, I know that but you said ... you didn't care about how I felt on things ...*

Dad: (said in a matter-of-fact way, not yelling) *I don't care about how you feel about things. I could give a damn about how you feel about things.*

Julie: *And that's ... I don't agree with that.*

Dad: *Well, I better drop that conversation, 'cause it don't have anything to do with me I don't think.*

This was not a heated conversation between Julie and her father. They did not raise their voices at each other and, for most of the conversation, Julie had a soft smile across her face. This is a perfect example of the typical conversations we have day in and day out with family, significant others, friends, and coworkers. Yet, when we take a deeper look at the conversation there are many things going on that we don't always pick up on, because we weren't taught how to dissect communication and look at the underlying messages.

Let's now evaluate it from an emotional intelligence perspective. We'll look beyond the words and instead assess the potential feelings both Julie and her father were trying to convey (but failed to).

Dad: *Well, smile Julie.*

(This statement is a command. Julie's father may have just wanted reassurance that she was happy. To Julie, this command to smile may have made her feel like he didn't understand how she was feeling, or he didn't care. To serve his needs *and* Julie's, he might

have said instead, "Julie, I notice you're not smiling. That concerns me because I want you to be happy. Are you not happy?")

Julie: *I'm not real happy.*

(Julie expresses her feelings, indicating why she isn't smiling.)

Dad: *Durn if you don't look happy.*

(Instead of taking the opportunity to ask why she wasn't happy, Julie's dad makes an accusation that her actions don't seem to match her words).

Julie: *I don't know, I don't think you realize you're not going to see me for a while.*

(Julie may be trying to give her dad an opportunity to understand why she isn't happy while also wanting confirmation he will miss her.)

[gap in conversation]

Dad: *Well, don't you think we think alike?*

Julie: *No, I don't at all.*

Dad: *Well, where do we differ? Well, I'd probably like to know.*

(It seems that Julie's dad really wants to come from a place of understanding and relate to his daughter. He also may not see how different they really are.)

Julie: *Where do we differ?*

(By reiterating the question, Julie may be implying her shock that her father would even ask how they differ. To her, their differences seem very apparent.)

Dad: *Yes.*

Julie: (smiling) *I think that it's okay to wear whatever you want to wear ... and not cut your hair ... whereas you don't think that's okay.*

Dad: *... [G]o ahead, what else is it that you don't like about me?*

(In asking "What else is it that you don't like about me?" it's clear that Julie's dad is taking it personally that they disagree, instead of simply accepting they have different beliefs. Because he is more focused on himself being attacked (which isn't the case), he is less likely to hear his daughter's real needs.)

Julie: *I hate it that it took these people getting here [MTV camera crew] to make you listen to what anyone else has to say about anything. I just think it's very evident in the way that we think that there's a big age difference.*

(Julie is saying that she hasn't felt that she could express herself and her feelings to her father until now. She is also saying that their strongest disagreements seem to stem from a generation gap.)

Dad: *I, ugh, I still care about you honey. Did you know it?*

(Although he may not agree with his daughter, Julie's dad wants her to know that he cares about her. By asking, "Did you know it?" he seems to want reassurance that she knows he cares about her.)

Julie: *Well, I know that but you said ... you didn't care about how I felt on things ...*

(Julie gives him reassurance and then follows with a "but," which tends to void or put into question the prior statement. What Julie might be trying to say to her father is, "You say you care, and I feel you contradict yourself when, at other times, you say you don't care how I feel about things. For me, those two go hand-in-hand.")

Dad: (said in a matter-of-fact way, not yelling) *I don't care about how you feel about things. I could give a damn about how you feel about things.*

(Making this statement may have undone the relationship building that Julie's dad may have been trying to accomplish. His previous words of caring are drowned out by the dismissal of her emotions.)

Julie: *[A]nd that's ... I don't agree with that.*

(Julie seems to start an explanation, but leaves it at, "I don't agree with that," feeling hopeless in getting her dad to understand her logic and feelings.)

Dad: *Well, I better drop that conversation, 'cause it don't have anything to do with me I don't think.*

(Julie's dad feels he's involved in a losing battle and denies that he is the problem by stating, "'cause it don't have anything to do with me I don't think.")

How does reading this commentary alongside the dialogue between Julie and her father affect the way you think about communication?

_____

_____

_____

_____

_____

Where in your life do you now see hidden messages you didn't notice before?

_____

_____

_____

_____

_____

How might your life change if you begin applying EQ and effective communication strategies?

_____

_____

_____

_____

_____

We all have the ability to reverse the steady hike of anxiety, stress, depression, and outrage, while increasing compassion, understanding, and overall well-being. But first, we must be able to communicate beyond our emotions and decipher the hidden messages of others.

When we take the initiative to become more effective communicators, and convey our needs instead of projecting our emotions, we are on the path to becoming more emotionally intelligent. And when we are emotionally intelligent, we can be a catalyst for positive change and work towards eliminating *the EQ deficiency*.

15

You Can Be a Catalyst for Change

"Change will not come if we wait for some other person, or if we wait for some other time. We are the ones we've been waiting for. We are the change that we seek."

— **Barack Obama**

You may have heard of her. Greta Thunberg, a young Swedish environmental activist, born in 2003, has taken the world by storm. In 2018, at the age of 15, Greta addressed world leaders at the United Nations Climate Change Conference. Her speech was powerful and filled with conviction, emotion, and much data and research.

This young girl sparked awareness which caught the attention of millions around the globe. Movements began to form; people began to focus more on their own carbon footprint and support the cause for a cleaner and healthier planet.

Regardless of how you feel about Greta, she is a perfect example of how an ordinary individual, with strong convictions, can spark a movement for positive change.

Discomfort and strong feelings toward the lack of action was the driving force behind Greta's urge to act. When we feel discomfort and strong emotions, we can do one of two things: deflect and ignore, or act. Facing the truth is not easy, but ignoring the truth is far bleaker and more discomforting in the long run.

THE PROCESS OF CHANGE

Pain, despair, and unhappiness are often the driving forces behind change. Sometimes, like deciding to go to a doctor, we delay until we are in utter misery.

The process of change is not easy, and it can take time, but it will be worth it. It will take courage and test your patience at times. You will need to manage your energy and have compassion for yourself and others.

Change begins by asking yourself what you want. After deciding what is most important to you, you can focus on the elements of your life that either support or hinder your development. Start by asking yourself the following questions.

What do I want out of life?
Be sure to identify what you *want*, not what you *don't want*.
Example: I want to reduce my stress and anxiety.

_____

_____

_____

_____

_____

What in my life is not supporting my needs?

_____

_____

_____

_____

_____

_____

What is the most important change that I need to make?

_____

_____

_____

_____

What do I need to do to support this change?

_____

_____

_____

_____

On a scale of 1-10, with 1 being very little and 10 being very much, how much would this change impact your life?

[ ]

Using the same scale, how commited are you to this change?

[ ]

OLD HABITS DIE HARD

Habits are near impossible to break overnight due to the strong neural circuitry we have built around those habits. For example, parents who are not usually the ones taking their children to day care can find themselves driving straight to work with their child fast asleep in the back seat of the car.

We often do not recall our commutes to work, the words that come out of our mouths, how much water we drink daily, and whether we bite our nails or play with our hair. Such habits are arguably the most difficult to break, partly because they run at a subconscious level in our minds, and partly because there appears to be no major "cost" involved in maintaining the habit. For example, what is the worst that could happen from constantly fidgeting with your hair?

However, subconscious habits like eye rolls, negative tone, closed-off body language, biases, and negative self-talk can throw a wrench in the gears of positive change. It is important for us to become aware of these subconscious habits through self-awareness and by soliciting feedback from others.

FOCUS ON YOU

It's easy for us to identify the faults of others while failing to see that same fault within ourselves. Similarly, it's much easier to try and convince someone else they need to change before we think of taking it upon ourselves to be the change that we wish to see in the world. However, when we take the initiative to change ourselves first, we pave the way for others to follow suit.

Who Wants Change? Who Wants to Change?

Change occurs when we stop looking for change to take place outside ourselves and take the initiative to be the catalyst for change.

In the case of emotional intelligence, it is more than simply deciding we are going to change; emotional intelligence is a skill that needs to be developed. First, we need to identify our current stage of competence.

COMPETENCE CYCLE

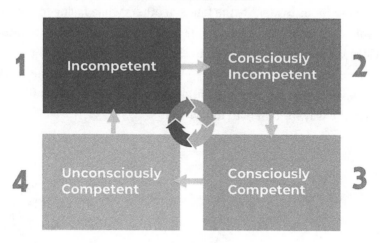

1. Incompetent: A State of Ignorance

Contrary to popular belief, being ignorant does not make us idiots. We simply do not know what we do not know. Even Einstein, as a toddler, had to be taught not to put his hand on a hot stove. Incompetence is the stage we must all step out of before we can learn; we have to become aware of new information to develop a new skill.

Before humans understood the importance of hygiene and its correlation with the spread of disease, the world was a much filthier place. We look back at the medieval ages, with its kings and queens, and how glamorously the era is depicted in fairy tales, and we may think what an enchanting time it must have been to live in. But this would be completely disregarding the fact that human waste was dumped out of windows onto the streets, where horses and other animals defecated, and regular bathing and sterilization were uncommon.

You've probably seen the disgust on people's faces when they catch a whiff of someone who hasn't bathed in a month; you can imagine their reaction if they were to see someone toss their bodily waste out of their front door, into the streets. But, back then, such behavior was normal. The people of the medieval era were ignorant regarding proper sanitation and healthy hygiene.

Today, we are a "smelly" bunch when it comes to our lack of emotional intelligence. Close to 90% of the population is completely ignorant of their lack of self-awareness and their inability to regulate their emotions. However, as we've seen in this book, most people were never taught *how* to think, feel, and react to others. With that education, we can move out of the incompetence phase (being unaware and ignorant) to the conscious incompetence phase.

2. Consciously Incompetent: A State of Awareness

Conscious incompetence is the state of awareness. Information has presented itself to us, and we now understand the importance of obtaining a new skill set. However, knowing is not doing. During the phase of conscious incompetence, we have been informed or made aware, but we have not yet put this new information into practice.

Attending a seminar is a good example of attaining conscious incompetence. The attendees are merely observers and note takers in the process. Awareness is a *huge* step in the process of change. Every skill we have ever learned started with first being aware. Now comes the challenge.

3. Consciously Competent: Actively Practicing

Phase three is the most challenging phase. Learning a new skill or changing an existing behavior takes hard work and consistent practice. Professional athletes and musicians are graceful and fluid at their craft because they have spent extensive amounts of time training in their discipline. As we develop conscious competence—in relation to emotional intelligence—we learn how to:

- Be mindful of ourselves and our surroundings.
- Regulate our emotions.
- Identify and eliminate intolerances.
- Apply techniques to reduce stress and anxiety.
- Refrain from acting on our impulses.
- Recognize and redirect our bias.
- Become more conscious of how we communicate and interpret the communication of others.
- Demonstrate empathy and understanding.

During this phase, there will be inevitable setbacks; that is okay and to be expected. Some days will be better than others. The key is not to become discouraged. Unceasing practice and repetition are the foundation, but self-compassion is also a necessity at this stage of growth and development.

An example: recall how you felt when you first sat in the driver's seat in a car. Do you recall how strange it felt when you first took to the open road? The first time behind the wheel can be stressful. It may have been difficult to gauge how close the passenger tire was to the shoulder of the road. You may have taken turns more slowly or felt you could easily lose control and skid off the road. But, with practice, you became increasingly comfortable behind the wheel.

If you have ever made it from point A to point B without recalling the details of your commute, you have successfully reached the next and final phase of competence: unconscious competence.

4. Unconsciously Competent: Actively Practicing

Once we have achieved unconscious competence, "doing" is as simple as breathing. We don't even have to think about it. We have practiced to the point that our new skill has become second nature to us. It is impossible to master any skill with just a few hours (even weeks or months) of practice. At best, in the beginning, we will reach conscious competence if we apply what we have learned. Truly unconscious competence takes a lot of time and effort to achieve.

Even if we never reach the level of unconscious competence, we should not feel discouraged. Conscious competence is a wonderful place to be; its results are noticeable and life changing. The advantage of unconscious competence, however, is the amount of energy we save when applying our new skill. For example, when we were children, learning to dress ourselves was likely exhausting. Now we can slip on our clothes in the dark if we need to, with little energy and thought. In the area of dressing ourselves, we've achieved unconscious competence.

COMMITTED TO THE CHANGE

Every step toward our goal, no matter how small, is progress. Never beat yourself up because you do not notice a difference. You would be surprised at how these little changes add up to big results. Gary Keller's book, *The One Thing,* explains how one domino can knock down a domino 1.5 times its size. By the 23rd domino, a single tiny domino can initiate a reaction that brings down a domino the size of the Eiffel Tower. By the 57th, it will topple a domino as tall as the distance from the Earth to the Moon.

When mastering any skill, focus on one habit or behavior at a time. Do not overwhelm yourself with too many changes at once. For example, if your goal is to change the way you react during stressful situations, the first step might be to develop an awareness of your triggers. Be mindful—present and nonjudgmental—of all the sensations, thoughts, and feelings that arise during stressful circumstances.

There are many great ways to observe your incremental changes turning into big results. Keeping a daily journal is one of them and I highly encourage it. Journaling allows us to uncover our own hidden messages and can bring to light many of the unconscious biases, thoughts, and feelings we allow to get in our own way. A few suggestions when journaling to develop emotional intelligence are:

- Record how you feel throughout your day. Notice what emotions you feel, what you were thinking or experiencing when feeling those emotions, and how you reacted.

- If possible, journal while in your current state of mind, even if it feels like your emotions are out of control or experiencing stress or anger. Do not worry about how it sounds or comes across. The more transparent the better.

- When journaling in an unpleasant emotional state, record how you transitioned into a more positive state. How long did it take? What changed?

- Make the effort to review old entries to observe your mindset shifts, growth, and identify patterns and underlying needs. Just like a sports team reviews footage from the previous game to analyze what they did well and areas they can improve upon, rereading journal entries are like watching a playback of your thoughts and reactions with a greater sense of clarity. It will provide you with a huge amount of insight.

- The more documentation you have, the better. However, anything is better than nothing. At the very least, I recommend a paragraph summary of your day and a list of the main three moods you experienced.

You may be surprised at just how valuable tracking your thoughts, feelings, and reactions are to developing a higher emotional intelligence.

FINAL WORDS

I believe in you. You are reading this book because you wish to increase your emotional intelligence or feel concerned about the state of humanity. I believe you are going to be a catalyst for change by becoming a highly emotionally intelligent being and applying your skills to better your life and the lives of others. You can be the domino that sets into motion a beautiful chain reaction of self-compassion and understanding, reducing your stress and anxiety while igniting a spark of positive emotion that spreads to the people around you.

This world is a dark place only if we choose to keep our eyes closed.

PERSONAL CHANGE AGREEMENT:

If you're committed to making a personal change after reading this book, then sign this agreement, tear it out, and put it somewhere you will see it. Feel free to make copies of it before you sign it, so you may share it with others.

I _____, realize I have the power to be a catalyst for positive change in this world. It is *my* willingness to come from a place of genuine understanding and take full responsibility for *my* thoughts and behaviors that will evoke change; not empty words and promise or the expectation of others to change.

I honorably hold myself accountable to be a person who:

- Takes the time to know thy true self; developing a deep understanding for my purpose and objectively identifying and accepting my flaws and strengths with self-compassion, so that I might show that same appreciation and understanding for others.
- Approaches every situation with an awareness that my perspective is only one puzzle piece of reality.
- Acknowledges that behind every unpleasant emotion there is an unmet need and purpose. It is our responsibility as emotionally intelligent change agents to help identify that need within ourselves and others.
- Is patient with myself and others, knowing that change takes time. I will not allow setbacks to prevent me from moving forward in my journey to be a more emotionally intelligent being.

All this, I promise myself.

Sign: _____

Date: _____

Acknowledgements

Like limiting the guest list for your wedding, it's hard to know where to draw the line with acknowledgements. So many people were involved in the process of writing this book. Mostly, indirectly providing their support and a listening ear when I needed to vent my concerns or talk through ideas.

First, I would like to acknowledge those who were directly involved in the writing process. To my editors Steven Rigolosi and Sarah Busby, you both were invaluable in this process. As a first-time author, I had many questions and self-doubt about writing this book. From the beginning, you both reassured me what I was feeling was natural and you had my back. It was a painless and enjoyable experience working with the both of you and I thank you for your contribution in making this book something I am proud of sharing with the world.

To Daryl, Kevin, and Julie, thank you for taking the time to speak with me and allowing me to share your wisdom and experiences in this book.

To my husband, thank you for believing in me, listening to my frustrations, and loving me—truly—unconditionally. The ability to maintain my sanity throughout this process is largely in part thanks to you.

To my parents, undeniably, I would not be where I am today if it wasn't for the two of you. Thank you for always believing in me and seeing my potential, even in times when I could not.

To my friend Andrew, you may not like this comparison, but, you were one of my biggest cheerleaders. When I was down on myself, you always offered words of encouragement. I thank you for your friendship and being someone I can count on.

Next, my mentors (Dr. dePhillips, Brian, and Dr.Frost) who have been in my corner long before this book was in the making. Thank you all for your wisdom and continuous support.

To my beta readers, your feedback was essential to ensuring this book is a success. Thank you for your selfless time and insight.

And finally, to anyone who has not been named but supports my mission; to all of you reading this book, and to every change agent out there who is taking it upon themselves to make the world a better place, I thank you.

Work Consulted

A (Very) Brief History of Government. A (Very) Brief History of Government. (2012). https://2012books.lardbucket.org/books/a-primer-on-politics/s03-03-a-very-brief-history-of-govern.html.

21, M. (2019, March 22). *Big Gods Came After the Rise of Civilizations, Not Before, Study Finds.* UConn Today. https://today.uconn.edu/2019/03/big-gods-came-rise-civilizations-not-study-finds/.

Ali Salah, A., Gevers, T., Sebe, N., & Vinciarelli, A. (2010). salah10challenges. Amsterdam; Institute of Informatics, University of Amsterdam.

Challenges of Human Behavior Understanding
Antidepressant Market: Growth, Trends, and Forecasts (2020-2025). Market Research - Consulting, Reports, Advisory, Sizing. https://www.mordorintelligence.com/industry-reports/antidepressants-market.

Armour, J. A. *Chapter 01: Heart-Brain Communication.* HeartMath Institute. https://www.heartmath.org/research/science-of-the-heart/heart-brain-communication/.

Asma, S. T., & Gabriel, R. (2020, June 7). *Human culture and cognition evolved through the emotions – Stephen T Asma & Rami Gabriel: Aeon Essays.* Aeon. https://aeon.co/essays/human-culture-and-cognition-evolved-through-the-emotions.

Banda, T. (2012). *3 Big Social Media Stats Every SMB Should Know.* Business 2 Community. https://www.business2community.com/social-media/3-big-social-media-stats-every-smb-should-know-0266973.

Barberá, P. (2015). barbera-tpbw. New York; New York University.

Bradberry, Travis. "14 Signs That You're Incredibly Emotionally Intelligent - and a High Performer." *Business Insider*, Business Insider, 31 Oct. 2019, www.businessinsider.com/high-performers-emotionally-intelligent-signs-2019-4.

Berkowitz , B., & Alcantara, C. (2019). *More than 50 years of U.S. mass shootings: The victims, sites, killers and weapons.* The Washington Post. https://www.washingtonpost.com/graphics/2018/national/mass-shootings-in-america/.

Bozi, R. (2017, March 11). *Category: brain and development.* Brilliant Healing Systems. https://brillianthealingsystems.com/?cat=18.

Brooking, E. T., & Singer, P. W. (2016, October 11). *War Goes Viral.* The Atlantic. https://www.theatlantic.com/magazine/archive/2016/11/war-goes-viral/501125/.

Brown, D. (2017, August 20). *How One Man Convinced 200 Ku Klux Klan Members To Give Up Their Robes.* NPR. https://www.npr.org/2017/08/20/544861933/how-one-man-convinced-200-ku-klux-klan-members-to-give-up-their-robes.

Cable News Network. (2019, November 28). *Deadliest Mass Shootings in Modern US History Fast Facts.* CNN. https://www.cnn.com/2013/09/16/us/20-deadliest-mass-shootings-in-u-s-history-fast-facts//.

Carroll, L. (2020, February 25). *12 Truths About Defensive Behavior.* mindbodygreen. https://www.mindbodygreen.com/0-17713/12-truths-about-defensive-behavior.html.

Cerroni-Long, E. L. (2000). *Anthropological theory in North America.* Bergin & Garvey.

Charlton, D. (2019, May 20). *This Invisible Problem Is Costing Employers $500 Billion Per Year.* Inc.com. https://www.inc.com/don-charlton/this-invisible-problem-is-costing-employers-500-billion-per-year.html.

Cherry, K. (2020, April 30). *Is It Possible to Overcome Implicit Bias?* Verywell Mind. https://www.verywellmind.com/implicit-bias-overview-4178401.

Childre, D. L., & Cryer, B. (2004). *From chaos to coherence: the power to change performance.* Planetary.

Cognitive Bias - Examples, List of Top 10 Types of Biases. Corporate Finance Institute. (2020, January 16). https://corporatefinanceinstitute.com/resources/knowledge/trading-investing/list-top-10-types-cognitive-bias/.

Cook, S. (2020). *Cyberbullying Statistics and Facts for 2020.* Comparitech. https://www.comparitech.com/internet-providers/cyberbullying-statistics/.

Cooper-White, M. (2014, August 15). *Religious Beliefs, Emotional Problems Linked In Provocative New Study.* HuffPost. https://www.huffpost.com/entry/religion-mental-health-angry-god-brain_n_3097025.

Cortisol. You and Your Hormones. https://www.yourhormones.info/hormones/cortisol/.

Coviello, L., Sohn, Y., Kramer, A. D. I., Marlow, C., Franceschetti, M., Christakis, N. A., & Fowler, J. H. (2014). Detecting Emotional Contagion in Massive Social Networks. *PLoS ONE, 9*(3). https://doi.org/10.1371/journal.pone.0090315

Cuncic, A. (2019, July 17). *What Happens to Your Body When You're Thinking?* Verywell Mind. https://www.verywellmind.com/what-happens-when-you-think-4688619.

Dedaj, P. (2019, January 22). *Video shows students in confrontation with Native Americans, prompting apology from Catholic diocese, high school.* Fox News. https://www.foxnews.com/politics/video-shows-students-allegedly-mocking-native-american-elder-veteran.

DeLaplante, Kevin, director. *The Dangers of Tribalism.* YouTube: The Dangers of Tribalism, 2018, www.youtube.com/watch?v=7y-b7f6CK2M&t=3s. Accessed 2020.

Dispenza, J. (2009). *Evolve your brain: the science of changing your mind.* Health Communications.

Dodgson, L. (2017, December 19). *Our brains sometimes create 'false memories' - but science suggests we could be better off this way.* Business Insider. https://www.businessinsider.com/science-of-false-memories-2017-12.

Donegan, R. (2012). Bullying and Cyberbullying: History, Statistics, Law, Prevention and Analysis. *The Elon Journal of Undergraduate Research in Communications, Vol. 3*(Spring 2012), 33–42.

Dwyer, C. (2018, September 7). *12 Common Biases That Affect How We Make Everyday Decisions.* Psychology Today. https://www.psychologytoday.com/us/blog/thoughts-thinking/201809/12-common-biases-affect-how-we-make-everyday-decisions.

Entis, L. (2017, March 22). *Chronic Loneliness Is a Modern-Day Epidemic.* Fortune. https://fortune.com/2016/06/22/loneliness-is-a-modern-day-epidemic/.

Eurich, T. (2018, April 23). *What Self-Awareness Really Is (and How to Cultivate It).* Harvard Business Review. https://hbr.org/2018/01/what-self-awareness-really-is-and-how-to-cultivate-it.

Forsythe, F. (2018, September 17). *6 Things That Hide Behind Defensive Behavior and How to Deal with It.* Learning Mind. https://www.learning-mind.com/defensive-behavior/.

Freifeld, L. (2019, February 28). *2018 Training Industry Report.* Training Magazine. https://trainingmag.com/trgmag-article/2018-training-industry-report/.

Gasior, M. (2017, November 18). Why Is Compliance Training Important?: How to create a high-impact compliance training program. https://www.powerdms.com/blog/why-is-compliance-training-important/.

Goleman, D. (2006). *Emotional intelligence*. Bantam Books.

Green, R. *The Emotional Intelligence Institute - What is emotional intelligence? - 4. Mayer and Salovey model of emotional intelligence*. The Emotional Intelligence Institute - What is emotional intelligence? - 4. Mayer and Salovey model of emotional intelligence. http://www.theeiinstitute.com/what-is-emotional-intelligence/4-mayer-and-salovey-model-of-emotional-intelligence.html.

Haak, E. (2017, November 10). *A Yale Neuroscientist on Outrage in the Social Media Age*. Thrive Global. https://thriveglobal.com/stories/a-yale-neuroscientist-on-outrage-in-the-social-media-age/.

Hagerty, A. M. (2019, March 26). *Teen accused of shooting inside Concord Mills theater over seating dispute in custody*. https://www.wbtv.com. https://www.wbtv.com/2019/03/24/police-investigating-shooting-inside-concord-mills-mall/.

Haidt, J., & Haidt, J. D. (2005). *Wired to be Inspired*. Greater Good. https://greatergood.berkeley.edu/article/item/wired_to_be_inspired.

Headbloom, A. (2015, August 25). *Stereotypes vs. Generalizations*. feel like you belong. http://feellikeyoubelong.com/whats-up-blog/2015/8/24/stereotypes-vs-generalizations.

Headbloom, Alan. "Stereotypes vs. Generalizations." *Feel like You Belong*, Feel like You Belong, 25 Aug. 2015, feellikeyoubelong.com/whats-up-blog/2015/8/24/stereotypes-vs-generalizations.

Hiscott, R. (2014, March 14). *8 Ways Tech Has Completely Rewired Our Brains*. Mashable. https://mashable.com/2014/03/14/tech-brains-neuroplasticity/.

Howley, E. K. (2018, September 5). *How Communications Issues Between Doctors and Nurses Can Affect Your Health*. U.S. News & World Report. https://health.usnews.com/health-care/patient-advice/articles/2018-09-05/how-communications-issues-between-doctors-and-nurses-can-affect-your-health.

Impact of Fear and Anxiety. Taking Charge of Your Health & Wellbeing. (2016). https://www.takingcharge.csh.umn.edu/impact-fear-and-anxiety.

Khan, A. (2016, February 10). *Belief in all-knowing, punitive gods aided the growth of human societies, study says*. Los Angeles Times. https://www.latimes.com/science/sciencenow/la-sci-sn-gods-punishment-society-spread-20160210-story.html.

King, B. J. (2012, September 13). *For How Long Have We Been Human?* NPR. https://www.npr.org/sections/13.7/2012/09/11/160934187/for-how-long-have-we-been-human.

Kingsley, D. (2018, January 3). *A Revolution in Human Consciousness*. Kingsley L. Dennis. https://kingsleydennis.com/a-revolution-in-human-consciousness/.

Kinney, T., & Kinney, M. T. (2020, February 12). *The Organizational Cost of Low Emotional Intelligence in the Workplace*. HPISolutions. https://hpisolutions.com/the-organizational-cost-of-low-emotional-intelligence-in-the-workplace/.

Komo Staff. (2019, June 14). *Father 'executed' his daughter over a 'petty argument' about a baby gate, prosecutor says*. WBMA. https://abc3340.com/news/nation-world/father-executed-his-daughter-over-a-petty-argument-about-a-baby-gate-prosecutor-says-06-14-2019.

Komo. (2019, June 27). *Man charged with killing daughter in dispute over baby gate pleads not guilty.* KOMO. https://komonews.com/news/local/man-charged-with-killing-daughter-in-dispute-over-baby-gate-pleads-not-guilty.

Kristine Phillips, C. W. (2019, January 23). *Catholic school teen in viral video: 'Now I wish I would have walked away'.* The Washington Post. https://www.washingtonpost.com/nation/2019/01/23/catholic-school-teen-viral-video-now-i-wish-i-would-have-walked-away/.

Learning, L. *Introduction to Sociology.* Lumen. https://courses.lumenlearning.com/sociology/chapter/stereotypes-prejudice-and-discrimination/.

Leary, M. (2017, June 29). *Most Problems Are People Problems.* Psychology Today. https://www.psychologytoday.com/us/blog/toward-less-egoic-world/201706/most-problems-are-people-problems.

Lejuwaan, J. (2010). *How Your Thoughts Program Your Cells.* HighExistence. https://highexistence.com/thoughts-program-cells/.

Lerner, H. (2013, November 10). *Stop Being So Defensive!* Psychology Today. https://www.psychologytoday.com/us/blog/the-dance-connection/201311/stop-being-so-defensive.

Lewis, T. (2018, September 28). *Human Brain: Facts, Functions & Anatomy.* LiveScience. https://www.livescience.com/29365-human-brain.html.

Lieberman , D. E. (2013). *The Story of the Human Body: Evolution, Health, and ...* https://www.amazon.com/Story-Human-Body-Evolution-Disease-ebook/dp/B00C8S9VCK.

The limbic system. Queensland Brain Institute. (2019, January 24). https://qbi.uq.edu.au/brain/brain-anatomy/limbic-system.

Lopez, G., & Sukumar, K. (2018, July 9). *Mass shootings since Sandy Hook, in one map.* Vox.com. https://www.vox.com/a/mass-shootings-america-sandy-hook-gun-violence.

Los Angeles Times. (2019, June 18). *Suicide rates for U.S. teens and young adults are the highest on record.* Los Angeles Times. https://www.latimes.com/science/la-sci-suicide-rates-rising-teens-young-adults-20190618-story.html.

Los Angeles Times. (2019, September 1). *Opinion: We analyzed 53 years of mass shooting data. Attacks aren't just increasing, they're getting deadlier.* Los Angeles Times. https://www.latimes.com/opinion/story/2019-09-01/mass-shooting-data-odessa-midland-increase.

Martinovich, M. (2017, October 6). *Change behaviors by changing perception of normal.* Stanford News. https://news.stanford.edu/2017/10/06/change-behaviors-changing-perception-normal/.

Marusak, J., & Douglas, A. (2020). *'It could be your child.' In Charlotte, shootings - some murders - start with petty fights.* charlotteobserver. https://www.charlotteobserver.com/news/local/crime/article235706817.html.

Maslin, M. (2019). *Here Are Five of The Most Common Climate Change Misconceptions, Debunked.* ScienceAlert. https://www.sciencealert.com/here-s-what-the-science-says-about-five-common-climate-change-myths.

Mccraty, R., Barrios-Choplin, B., Rozman, D., Atkinson, M., & Watkins, A. D. (1998). The impact of a new emotional self-management program on stress, emotions, heart rate variability, DHEA and cortisol. *Integrative Physiological and Behavioral Science, 33*(2), 151–170. https://doi.org/10.1007/bf02688660

McGovern Institute For Brain Research, Massachusetts Institute Of Technology (MIT). (2009, July 30). *Adult Brain Can Change Within Seconds.* ScienceDaily. Retrieved June 6, 2020 from www.sciencedaily.com/releases/2009/07/090714203442.htm

Milgram, S. (1963). Behavioral Study of obedience. *The Journal of Abnormal and Social Psychology, 67*(4), 371–378. https://doi.org/10.1037/h0040525

Moss, D. S. (2016). *Moral elevation.* Sicotests. https://www.sicotests.com/psyarticle.asp?id=262.

Murphy, K. (2013, October 19). *Ma'am, Your Burger Has Been Paid For.* The New York Times. https://www.nytimes.com/2013/10/20/opinion/sunday/maam-your-burger-has-been-paid-for.html.

Nadler, R. (2011, November 16). *Steve Jobs: Superman Syndrome, Low EQ, High IQ.* Psychology Today. https://www.psychologytoday.com/us/blog/leading-emotional-intelligence/201111/steve-jobs-superman-syndrome-low-eq-high-iq.

Neville, S. *Emotional hijack.* Emotional hijack. https://www.alchemyassistant.com/topics/PaT4j2YKrTSMGkN5.html.

Noriega, D., & Owen, T. (2019, November 19). *Nearly All Mass Shooters Since 1966 Have Had 4 Things in Common.* Vice. https://www.vice.com/en_us/article/a35mya/nearly-all-mass-shooters-since-1966-have-had-four-things-in-common.

NPR. (2019, October 7). *Screaming Into The Void: How Outrage Is Hijacking Our Culture, And Our Minds.* NPR. https://www.npr.org/transcripts/767186846.

O'Connell, C. (2020, March 21). *15 Ordinary People Who Changed History.* Reader's Digest. https://www.rd.com/true-stories/inspiring/inspiring-stories-9-ordinary-people-who-changed-history/.

Ortiz, J. L. (2019, January 24). *Fuller video casts new light on Covington Catholic students' encounter with Native American elder.* USA Today. https://www.usatoday.com/story/news/2019/01/20/covington-catholic-students-full-video-shows-viral-protest-new-light/2635085002/.

Ortiz-Ospina, E. (2019). *The rise of social media.* Our World in Data. https://ourworldindata.org/rise-of-social-media.

Parrish, M. (2007, November 1). *10-Year-Old With Matches Started a California Wildfire.* https://www.nytimes.com/2007/11/01/us/01wildfire.html.

Paul, A. M. (1998, May 1). *Where Bias Begins: The Truth About Stereotypes.* Psychology Today. https://www.psychologytoday.com/us/articles/199805/where-bias-begins-the-truth-about-stereotypes.

Pearce, F. (2016, February 10). *Belief in punitive gods linked with expansion of human societies.* New Scientist. https://www.newscientist.com/article/2077082-belief-in-punitive-gods-linked-with-expansion-of-human-societies/.

ProjectImplicit. About the IAT. https://implicit.harvard.edu/implicit/iatdetails.html.

Purzycki, B. G., Apicella, C., Atkinson, Q. D., Cohen, E., Mcnamara, R. A., Willard, A. K., … Henrich, J. (2016). Moralistic gods, supernatural punishment and the expansion of human sociality. *Nature, 530*(7590), 327–330. https://doi.org/10.1038/nature16980

r/atheism - How Many People Have Been Killed in the Name of Religion? reddit. (2015). https://www.reddit.com/r/atheism/comments/33tofh/how_many_people_have_been_killed_in_the_name_of/.

Ray Sipherd, special to C. N. B. C. (2018, February 28). *The third-leading cause of death in US most doctors don't want you to know about.* CNBC. https://www.cnbc.com/2018/02/22/medical-errors-third-leading-cause-of-death-in-america.html.

Reed, P. (2019, June 22). *Does Excessive Screen Time Cause ADHD?* Psychology Today. https://www.psychologytoday.com/us/blog/digital-world-real-world/201906/does-excessive-screen-time-cause-adhd.

Roiphe, A. (1973, February 18). *"An American Family"*. The New York Times. https://www.nytimes.com/1973/02/18/archives/things-are-keen-but-could-be-keener-an-american-family-an-american.html.

Rosenblatt, D. J. (2019). *More screen time linked to higher risk of ADHD in preschool-aged children: Study*. ABC News. https://abcnews.go.com/Health/screen-time-linked-higher-risk-adhd-preschool-aged/story?id=62429157.

Rosenburg, M. B. (2003). *Nonviolent Communication a Language of Life 2nd ed ...* https://www.cnvc.org/. https://www.powells.com/book/nonviolent-communication-a-language-of-life-2nd-edition-9781892005038.

Roser, M., Ritchie, H., & Ortiz-Ospina, E. (2015, July 14). *Internet*. Our World in Data. https://ourworldindata.org/internet.

Schmidt, M. S. (2014, September 25). *F.B.I. Confirms a Sharp Rise in Mass Shootings Since 2000*. The New York Times. https://www.nytimes.com/2014/09/25/us/25shooters.html.

Soergel, A. (2017). *Is Social Media to Blame for Political Polarization in America?* U.S. News & World Report. https://www.usnews.com/news/articles/2017-03-20/is-social-media-to-blame-for-political-polarization-in-america.

Sorenson, Susan, and Keri Garman. "How to Tackle U.S. Employees' Stagnating Engagement." *Gallup.com*, Gallup, 6 Feb. 2020, news.gallup.com/businessjournal/162953/tackle-employees-stagnating-engagement.aspx.

staff, S. X. (2015, June 15). *Social structure matters in species conservation*. Phys.org. https://phys.org/news/2015-06-social-species.html.

Stress Can Increase Your Risk for Heart Disease. Content - Health Encyclopedia - University of Rochester Medical Center. https://www.urmc.rochester.edu/encyclopedia/content.aspx?ContentTypeID=1.

Sussex Publishers. *Motivated Reasoning*. Psychology Today. https://www.psychologytoday.com/us/basics/motivated-reasoning.

Suttie, J. (2018). *How Seeing the Good in People Can Help Bridge Our Differences*. Greater Good. https://greatergood.berkeley.edu/article/item/how_seeing_the_good_in_people_can_help_bridge_our_differences.

Szalavitz, M. (2011, October 20). *What Does a 400% Increase in Antidepressant Use Really Mean?* Time. https://healthland.time.com/2011/10/20/what-does-a-400-increase-in-antidepressant-prescribing-really-mean/.

Tariq, I. (2019, March 4). *Why More 'Emotional Intelligence' Means More Money for Entrepreneurs*. Entrepreneur. https://www.entrepreneur.com/article/327167.

TED. *Why I, as a Black Man, Attend KKK Rallies. | Daryl Davis | TEDxNaperville*. Performance by Daryl Davis, YouTube/Why I, as a Black Man, Attend KKK Rallies. | Daryl Davis | TEDxNaperville, TED, 2017, www.youtube.com/watch?v=ORp3q1Oaezw&t=84s.

Tucker, J. A., Guess, A., Barberá, P., Vaccari, C., Siegel, A., Sanovich, S., ... Nyhan, B. (2018). Social-Media-Political-Polarization-and-Political-Disinformation-Literature-Review.

Walinga, J., & Stangor, C. (2014, October 17). *1.2 The Evolution of Psychology: History, Approaches, and Questions*. Introduction to Psychology 1st Canadian Edition. https://opentextbc.ca/introductiontopsychology/chapter/1-2-the-evolution-of-psychology-history-approaches-and-questions/.

Walter, S. (2018, March 29). *Facebook and Instagram are 'killing off our memories'*. The Telegraph. https://www.telegraph.co.uk/news/2018/03/29/memories-altered-smartphone-photographs/.

What's Trending . (2017). *Taco Bell Drive-Thru Fight And Hangry Meltdown | What's Trending Now!* YouTube/Taco Bell Drive-Thru FIGHT And HANGRY MELTDOWN | What's Trending Now! https://www.youtube.com/watch?v=5XuqptddbGU.

Why 'bottling it up' can be harmful to your health. HCF. https://www.hcf.com.au/health-agenda/body-mind/mental-health/downsides-to-always-being-positive.

Wilford, J. N. (2002, February 26). *When Humans Became Human*. The New York Times. https://www.nytimes.com/2002/02/26/science/when-humans-became-human.html?auth=login-google.

Williamson, M. (2014, September 9). *The Revolution of Consciousness*. HuffPost. https://www.huffpost.com/entry/the-revolution-of-conscio_b_5574514.

Willis, J. K., & Ocean Portal Team. (2019, August 5). *Sea Level Rise*. Smithsonian Ocean. https://ocean.si.edu/through-time/ancient-seas/sea-level-rise.

Yuko, E. (2019, November 14). *10 Undeniable Facts About Mass Shootings in America*. Reader's Digest. https://www.rd.com/culture/facts-about-mass-shootings-in-america/.

Zimmerman, J. I. (2019, January 22). *I Failed the Covington Catholic Test*. The Atlantic. https://www.theatlantic.com/ideas/archive/2019/01/julie-irwin-zimmerman-i-failed-covington-catholic-test/580897/.

Chapter Notes:

[1] *In "Emotional Intelligence: New Ability or Eclectic Traits?" John D. Mayer, Peter Salovey and David R Caruso. American Psychologist, September 2008, Vol. 63, No.6, pages 503-517.*

[2] Information based on Daniel Goleman's summary of emotional intelligence.

[3] From Bradberry, Travis. "14 Signs That You're Incredibly Emotionally Intelligent - and a High Performer." *Business Insider*, Business Insider, 31 Oct. 2019, www.businessinsider.com/high-performers-emotionally-intelligent-signs-2019-4.

[4] From "Emotional Intelligence (EQ) Tests, Training, Certification & Coaching." *TalentSmart*, www.talentsmart.com/articles/Increasing-Your-Salary-with-Emotional-Intelligence-983916766-p-1.html.

[5] From Assistant Secretary for Public Affairs (ASPA). (2019, December 18). Facts About Bullying. Retrieved June 24, 2020, from https://www.stopbullying.gov/resources/facts

[6] From What's Trending . (2017). *Taco Bell Drive-Thru Fight And Hangry Meltdown | What's Trending Now! YouTube/Taco Bell Drive-Thru FIGHT And HANGRY MELTDOWN | What's Trending Now!* https

[7] From Oravetz, A. (2019, August 12). Man charged in deadly parking dispute pleads not guilty. Retrieved June 24, 2020, from https://www.9news.com/article/news/man-charged-in-deadly-parking-dispute-pleads-not-guilty/73-39286fa7-b188-4366-bb9b-6b0c55257dd1

[8] From Hagerty, A. (2019, March 26). Teen accused of shooting inside Concord Mills theater over seating dispute in custody. Retrieved June 24, 2020, from https://www.wbtv.com/2019/03/24/police-investigating-shooting-inside-concord-mills-mall/11

[9] From Reinstein, J. (2019, June 19). A Man Allegedly Fatally Shot His Daughter In Front Of Her Son Amid A "Petty" Fight About A Baby Gate. Retrieved June 24, 2020, from https://www.buzzfeednews.com/article/juliareinstein/man-shot-killed-daughter-over-baby-gate-argument

[10] From From Press, Associated. "Las Vegas Police Release Report on Lessons from 2017 Mass Shooting That Killed 58." *NBCNews.com*, NBCUniversal News Group, 11 July 2019, www.nbcnews.com/storyline/las-vegas-shooting/las-vegas-police-release-report-lessons-2017-mass-shooting-killed-n1028636; Blankstein, Andrew, et al. "Las Vegas Shooting: 59 Killed and More Than 500 Hurt Near Mandalay Bay." *NBCNews.com*, NBCUniversal News Group, 3 Oct. 2017, www.nbcnews.com/storyline/las-vegas-shooting/las-vegas-police-investigating-shooting-mandalay-bay-n806461.

[11] From Los Angeles Times. (2019, September 1). *Opinion: We analyzed 53 years of mass shooting data. Attacks aren't just increasing, they're getting deadlier.* Los Angeles Times. https://www.latimes.com/opinion/story/2019-09-01/mass-shooting-data-odessa-midland-increase.

[12] From Berkowitz , B., & Alcantara, C. (2019). *More than 50 years of U.S. mass shootings: The victims, sites, killers and weapons.* The Washington Post. https://www.washingtonpost.com/graphics/2018/national/mass-shootings-in-america/.

[13] From Noriega, D., & Owen, T. (2019, November 19). *Nearly All Mass Shooters Since 1966 Have Had 4 Things in Common.* Vice; Knoll, J. L., IV, & Annas, G. D. (2016). Mass Shootings and Mental Illness. Retrieved 2020, from https://psychiatryonline.org/doi/pdf/10.5555/appi.books.9781615371099

[14] From Knoll, J. L., IV, & Annas, G. D. (2016). Mass Shootings and Mental Illness. Retrieved 2020, from https://psychiatryonline.org/doi/pdf/10.5555/appi.books.9781615371099

[15] From Roiphe, A. (1973, February 18). *"An American Family".* The New York Times. https://www.nytimes.com/1973/02/18/archives/things-are-keen-but-could-be-keener-an-american-family-an-american.html.

[16] From Tschinkel, A. (2018). *So, here's the science behind why we're so obsessed with watching reality shows.* https://hellogiggles.com/reviews-coverage/tv-shows/science-behind-watching-reality-shows/.

[17] From Ortiz-Ospina, E. (2019). *The rise of social media.* Our World in Data. https://ourworldindata.org/rise-of-social-media.

[18] From *Number of people with anxiety disorders.* Our World in Data. https://ourworldindata.org/grapher/number-with-anxiety-disorders.

[19] From *Number of people with depression.* Our World in Data. https://ourworldindata.org/grapher/number-of-people-with-depression.

[20] From *r/atheism - How Many People Have Been Killed in the Name of Religion?* reddit. (2015).

[21] NPR. (2019, October 7). *Screaming Into The Void: How Outrage Is Hijacking Our Culture, And Our Minds.* NPR. https://www.npr.org/transcripts/767186846; Zimmerman, J. I. (2019, January 22). *I Failed the Covington Catholic Test.* The Atlantic. https://www.theatlantic.com/ideas/archive/2019/01/julie-irwin-zimmerman-i-failed-covington-catholic-test/580897/; Dedaj, P. (2019, January 22). *Video shows students in confrontation with Native Americans, prompting apology from Catholic diocese, high school.* Fox News. https://www.foxnews.com/politics/video-shows-students-allegedly-mocking-native-american-elder-veteran.

[22] From Pearce, F. (2016, February 10). *Belief in punitive gods linked with expansion of human societies.* New Scientist. https://www.newscientist.com/article/2077082-belief-in-punitive-gods-linked-with-expansion-of-human-societies/.

[23] From Purzycki, Benjamin Grant, et al. "Moralistic Gods, Supernatural Punishment and the Expansion of Human Sociality." *Nature*, vol. 530, no. 7590, 2016, pp. 327–330., doi:10.1038/nature16980.

[24] From Howley, E. K. (2018, September 5). *How Communications Issues Between Doctors and Nurses Can Affect Your Health.* U.S. News & World Report. https://health.usnews.com/health-care/patient-advice/articles/2018-09-05/how-communications-issues-between-doctors-and-nurses-can-affect-your-health.

[25] Reference endnote 21

[26] From Milgram, S. (1963). Behavioral Study of obedience. *The Journal of Abnormal and Social Psychology, 67*(4), 371–378. https://doi.org/10.1037/h0040525

[27] From Freifeld, L. (2019, February 28). *2018 Training Industry Report.* Training Magazine. https://trainingmag.com/trgmag-article/2018-training-industry-report/.

[28] From Sorenson, Susan, and Keri Garman. "How to Tackle U.S. Employees' Stagnating Engagement." *Gallup.com*, Gallup, 6 Feb. 2020, news.gallup.com/businessjournal/162953/tackle-employees-stagnating-engagement.aspx.

[29] From Gasior, M. (2017, November 18). Why Is Compliance Training Important?: How to create a high-impact compliance training program. https://www.powerdms.com/blog/why-is-compliance-training-important/.

[30] From Headbloom, Alan. "Stereotypes vs. Generalizations." *Feel like You Belong*, Feel like You Belong, 25 Aug. 2015, feellikeyoubelong.com/whats-up-blog/2015/8/24/stereotypes-vs-generalizations.

[31] From American Psychological Association. *APA Dictionary of Psychology*. American Psychological Association. https://dictionary.apa.org/ingroup-bias.

[32] From deLaplante, K. *The Dangers of Tribalism*. Argument Ninja Dojo. https://www.argumentninja.com/the-dangers-of-tribalism.

[33] From DeLaplante, Kevin, director. *The Dangers of Tribalism. YouTube: The Dangers of Tribalism*, 2018, www.youtube.com/watch?v=7y-b7f6CK2M&t=3s. Accessed 2020.

[34] From Lexico Dictionaries. *Groupthink: Definition of Groupthink by Oxford Dictionary on Lexico.com also meaning of Groupthink.* Lexico Dictionaries | English. https://www.lexico.com/en/definition/groupthink.

[35] From Nichols, T. M. (2019). *The death of expertise: the campaign against established knowledge and why it matters.* Oxford University Press.

[36] From Eurich, T. (2018, April 23). *What Self-Awareness Really Is (and How to Cultivate It).* Harvard Business Review. https://hbr.org/2018/01/what-self-awareness-really-is-and-how-to-cultivate-it; Eurich, T. (2018, December 11). *Working with People Who Aren't Self-Aware.* Harvard Business Review. https://hbr.org/2018/10/working-with-people-who-arent-self-aware.

[37] Lexico Dictionaries. *Mind: Definition of Mind by Oxford Dictionary on Lexico.com also meaning of Mind.* Lexico Dictionaries | English. https://www.lexico.com/en/definition/mind.

[38] From Markowsky, G. (2017, June 16). *Physiology.* Encyclopædia Britannica. https://www.britannica.com/science/information-theory/Physiology.

[39] From French, Chris (2017). "The John Maddox Prize Nomination for Elizabeth Loftus". *Skeptical Inquirer.* **41** (2): 20–23.

[40] Regarding the 30% reduced change of heart disease is from Monique Tello, M. D. (2019, March 6). *A positive mindset can help your heart.* Harvard Health Blog. https://www.health.harvard.edu/blog/a-positive-mindset-can-help-your-heart-2019021415999. All other information can be found throughout Childre, D. L., & Cryer, B. (2004). *From chaos to coherence: the power to change performance.* Planetary.

[41] From Tamana, S. K., Ezeugwu, V., Chikuma, J., Lefebvre, D. L., Azad, M. B., Moraes, T. J., ... Mandhane, P. J. (2019). *Screen-time is associated with inattention problems in preschoolers: Results from the CHILD birth cohort study.* PLOS ONE. https://doi.org/10.1371/journal.pone.0213995.

[42] Tamir, D. I., Templeton, E. M., Ward, A. F., & Zaki, J. (2018). Media usage diminishes memory for experiences. *Journal of Experimental Social Psychology, 76*, 161-168. https://doi.org/10.1016/j.jesp.2018.01.006

[43] From *Why 'bottling it up' can be harmful to your health.* HCF. https://www.hcf.com.au/health-agenda/body-mind/mental-health/downsides-to-always-being-positive.

[44] Gross, J. J., & Levenson, R. W. (1997). Hiding feelings: The acute effects of inhibiting negative and positive emotion. *Journal of Abnormal Psychology, 106*(1), 95–103. https://doi.org/10.1037/0021-843x.106.1.95

[45] Varies studies have been conducted by the HeartMath Institute. You can see various data that supports the text on their website: *Science of the Heart.* HeartMath Institute. (2020, June 4). https://www.heartmath.org/research/science-of-the-heart/.

[46] From Haidt, J., & Haidt, J. D. (2005). *Wired to be Inspired.* Greater Good. https://greatergood.berkeley.edu/article/item/wired_to_be_inspired.

[47] Reference Endnote 42

[48] American Psychological Association. *Children, Youth, Families and Socioeconomic Status.* American Psychological Association. https://www.apa.org/pi/ses/resources/publications/children-families.

[49] From Belludi, N. (2017, October 27). *Albert Mehrabian's 7-38-55 Rule of Personal Communication.* Right Attitudes. https://www.rightattitudes.com/2008/10/04/7-38-55-rule-personal-communication/.